Sikhs and Sikhism
A View with a Bias

Sikhs and Sikhism
A View with a Bias

I. J. Singh

Manohar
1994

ISBN : 81-7304-058-3

First Published 1994

© I.J. Singh, 1994

Published by
Ajay Kumar Jain
Manohar Publishers and Distributors
2/6 Ansari Road, Daryaganj
New Delhi - 110 002

Lasertypeset by
Datatime Associates
C-2/1 (FF), Church Compound,
Sukhdev Vihar,
New Delhi 110 025.

Printed at
Rajkamal Electric Press
B-35/9, G.T. Karnal Road
Delhi - 110 033

Contents

Preface

Of the many journeys that life requires, of the many places to visit and of the many pilgrimages that one must make, to travel within is to travel the furthest. It is the most lonely path, a never-ending one, yet incomparable and seductive in its winding loveliness; to paraphrase Frost, the woods are indeed lovely, dark and deep. One must travel within to understand and master what lies without.

The institutions that sustain us, whether religious or secular, define for us the world outside in terms of the universe within us.

The essays in this collection define an ordinary Sikh's journey into the mystery and reality of Sikhism while living in a predominantly non-Sikh milieu. Since a man, in many ways, is shaped by his heritage, these essays present one Sikh's meandering through the highways and byways of his heritage. A journey that is, at once, tortuous and arduous, endless yet satisfying, but above all, is a journey of love. The essays present a non-scholarly view of the Sikh way of life.

In these writings, therefore, rational, intellectual conceptualizations are avoided as an unnecessary indulgence; they are better left to scholars. The opinions expressed are my responsibility and are indicative of my biases, yearnings, defeats, successes and excesses. Hopefully, my views can be supported by references to sikh sources of authority—whether scriptural, historical or anecdotal; however, such authoritative underpinnings for the arguments presented are deliberately kept to a minimum.

The essence of writing is best expressed by T.S. Eliot:

"Common words exact without vulgarity, formal words precise but not pedantic." Many of the essays are somewhat terse, others are rambling. I wish they could have all been shorter for words should be weighed, not counted.

My mother taught me that the reality of religion transcends logic. From my father I learned to enjoy the intellectually rigorous approach to Sikhism. It took me half a life-time to realize that the appreciation and understanding of Sikhism requires that it be accosted both devotionally and analytically; either technique alone remains insufficient.

Thinking about these matters was not always easy or comfortable but in the end, it was satisfying. Living and working with friends and foes alike resulted in this effort. The former made it possible, the latter made it necessary; I am grateful to both. Jerry Barrier has been a most encouraging source of support. I deeply appreciate his kindness as well his generous "Introduction" to these essays.

The question must be asked: Why write? It is a luxury, a form of self-indulgence but it remains the most precise and economical way of examining oneself as minutely and microscopically as one's inclinations and talents allow. A good mirror can reflect with brutal honesty.

In many ways these essays are talks with my father and daughter that could not occur.

I.J. Singh
New York

1 January 1994

Introduction

My encounters with Sikhs and their religion have provided me with some of the most exciting and meaningful experiences of my personal and intellectual life. Often the same encounters, however, have been accompanied by frustration and tension, mixed with bewilderment at times engendered by the seemingly enormous gaps between how Sikhs view the world around them and my outsider's perspective.

This volume of essays deals with the type of issues that have enriched and occasionally confounded a general understanding of Sikhs in the modern world. Dr. I.J. Singh's honest discussions of tradition, current practices, and contemporary controversies marks a new departure in literature on the recent Sikh experience. Scholarly and quasi-scholarly studies on some of the topics abound, as does the polemical literature in the form of books and issues of important periodicals such as the *Sikh Review* and the *World Sikh News*. None, however, attempt to address such a wide range of the Sikh religion and lifestyle as his reflections. There is a parallel between the work of Teja Singh, M.A., a scholar and teacher in the 1920s, and the essays of Dr I.J. Singh, a self-trained commentator on the Sikh experience.[1] Both lived in transitional periods. Teja Singh wrote extensively to explain Sikhism to a broad audience while at the same time aiming much of his discussion at the many factions and controversial figures surrounding him within the Sikh community. I.J. Singh does the same. Those without prior or with only a limited knowledge of the Sikh heritage can learn much from his clearly written studies, but embedded within the essays is a very rich set of ideas and interpretations that should make sense to Sikhs in a variety of social and cultural settings.

The essays have grown out of I.J. Singh's attempt to deal with his own heritage while working and living within a cultural context quite different from his Punjabi roots. There have been several waves of Sikh immigrants in North America. The first group, in the thousands, primarily came to work in western Canada and along the west coast of America. They settled as farmers, transferring institutions from the Punjab, and adapting as best they could to a new culture. By the 1920s, severe limits on their constitutional and immigration rights led many of these Sikhs either to return to India or to loose much of their attachment to Punjabi culture and their religious traditions.[2] A second wave of immigration began in the late 1940s, students and professionals who settled and in many ways became American. Although aware of their religious roots, many of these Sikhs were not as concerned about symbols and the details of doctrine as were some of their compatriots in the Punjab who, for political and religious reasons, felt threatened and therefore had a need to police the boundaries separating them from other religions, particularly Hinduism. As the author indicates in the prologue, they developed a hybrid culture but remained in religion Sikh. There followed new generations of immigrations, with varied views of the past and a tendency to quarrel over politics and issues.

All these Sikhs, of whatever group and ideology, share to some extent the same concerns that I.J. Singh clearly voices in his essays. The first revolve around what it means to be a Sikh, to constantly search for truth and to evaluate a learned tradition against a changing backdrop of cultural and psychological challenge. There are distinct signposts and symbols, which he discusses (the Guru, the *Guru Granth Sahib*, the historical Gurus and teachers, physical and mental discipline), but often these are discussed and made flesh in very particular institutional

settings. Especially valuable are I.J. Singh's attempts to com-
pare Sikhism with other religions and his appeal, reflected in
several essays, that concern with boundaries and "true religion" do not get in the way of the basic humanity and sense of
service and love found in the early Sikh traditions. A second
section deals with Sikh practice, ranging from distinctive approaches to baptism and marriage to taboos on specific foods
and approaches to environment, sexuality, and race relations. A
third group deals with politics, either internal as demonstrated
often in struggles within gurdwaras, or the ongoing debate over
Khalistan and how Sikhism can be protected in particular
political settings.

Many Sikhs may not agree with some of I.J. Singh's assessments, but that really does not matter either to him or to the
overall value of the interpretations. The toleration and open-
ness expressed in his essays are necessary components of the
Sikh tradition. Without such attitudes, individual Sikhs and
organizations can never transcend parochial roots and rightly
claim Sikhism's place as a major world religion.[3] Hopefully, the
essays will challenge the community to rethink its divisions, its
past, and its options for the future.

For the more general audience, I.J. Singh introduces many
key components of the Sikh religion and culture in lay language. He does not claim to be a technically trained scholar of
Sikh religion, but his judgements make sense and reflect
decades of debating issues and making sense of sometimes
complex concepts and institutions. Whether in the form of a
sermon, as for instance "A Man for All Seasons", or a clear
evaluation of the nature of *parshad* and ritual, his discussions
should help make Sikhism more accessible to those outside the
faith.

Why write and publish such essays that are often personal?
The answer really lies in how I.J. Singh has handled the various
transitions in his life. One way to try to understand what has

been happening to him and Sikhs around him is to attempt to capture ideas and feelings in written form. By examining his own development, he has helped us all understand not only one individual but the culture, the conflicts, and the rich tradition inherent among Sikhs in North America today.

N. Gerald Barrier
Professor of History
University of Missouri
December 26, 1992

Notes

1. General intellectual issues reviewed in the proceedings of the Toronto Sikh Conference, *Sikh History and Religion*, ed. Joseph O'Connell, et al. (University of Toronto South Asia Centre, 1989).
2. Immigration and consequent challenges discussed in the essays in N.G. Barrier and Van Dusenbery, eds, *The Sikh Diaspora* (South Asia Publications, 1990). For monographic assessment of particular groups and time periods, see Bruce LaBrack, *The Sikhs of Northern California* (AMS, 1990) and Karen Leonard, *Making Ethnic Choices* (Temple University Press, 1992).
3. The challenges confronting modern Sikhism discussed in essays by specialists in Jack Hawley and Gurinder Singh Mann, eds *Studying the Sikhs* (SUNY Press, 1993).

Prologue and
a Little History

In this preamble there is a little nostalgia and some history. In a roundabout manner, it is also the *raison d'etre* for the essays that follow.

There have been three significant migrations of Sikhs to this country, and a fourth presence now. Sikhs came here before the turn of the century over a hundred years ago. This was brought home to me over thirty years ago when, driving around Portland, Oregon, I came across a sign, "Panjab Tavern." Curious, I went in. There was an old lady behind the bar. Obviously pleased to see a Sikh, she talked about her youth 50 years earlier when Sikhs had lived in that area. I found out that the wild West was not tamed by the likes of John Wayne alone; Sikhs had a hand in opening it, as also in the building of the Panama Canal. Good farmhands and excellent workers, almost all of these Sikhs moved to Canada or California, where the political climate was more hospitable and economic opportunities more plentiful. I met one of them in Portland. He had been in the United States over 50 years and was then an old man in his seventies, making a precarious living driving a popcorn wagon around town. He had not seen a Sikh in many years and insisted on taking me home for a typical Punjabi dinner. His *chappatties* were irregularly polygonal but I can still vividly recall his affection and pleasure.

Eighty or ninety years ago, the Sikh quest for an independent identity was not as well established. Also, most of the immigrant Sikhs were poorly educated and had little understanding of their own roots. Perhaps a rare one of these early arrivals survived as a recognizable Sikh, although they built some gurdwaras. They were poor and uneducated when they came but not uncaring for they spearheaded a significant rebellion against the British (the Ghadar Party) from this continent.

The second migration of Sikhs followed India's independence in 1947. After the second World War, the United States became preeminent, while opportunities in Great Britain started to dwindle. Instead of going to Britain for higher studies, many young Sikhs started coming to the United States, especially because of the fellowships and scholarships available here. This trend became particularly noticeable in the mid-fifties. I am part of that generation. Most of us were young and single. We were Sikhs because we came from Sikh families, many of us were products of Christian education. Certainly, systematic instruction in our Sikh roots was wanting in almost all of us. Add the fact that this country is large, a continent where most of us found ourselves isolated, as I did - a lone Sikh at a campus miles from anywhere.

As a result, many of these married non-Sikh fellow students and settled here. Very few remained recognizable Sikhs. Yet a few found in that situation a need and the opportunity to confront their own roots. Culturally they became successful hybrids but in religion, Sikh. These few saw that one does not value something until he has been deprived of it. They recognized the beauty of their very liberal, pragmatic and progressive heritage, and realized that to be a good Sikh and a good American were not mutually exclusive ideas. I am one of that generation and these essays are the result.

The third wave of Sikhs started coming here in the mid-sixties when immigration quotas were relaxed, but most of them were already established professionals and businessmen in India. They came with their families to seek better opportunities. They came not because they had to but because they chose to. That fact alone delineates them from many of the other immigrants to this country. These Sikh families built the institutions and the gurdwaras that we see today but their needs are different. They have transplanted the Sikhism that they knew in India to this country but have rarely had to come to grips with their roots as the Sikhs of the second surge.

Now we are dealing with a fourth presence which again has two parts with very divergent needs. There are the young people, the children of the second and the third waves who were born or, at least, primarily raised here. Many of them have a better sense of the religion of their neighbors—and Christianity in all their hues — than of the one of their forefathers. Their approach to Sikhism is also different. They think differently. They are not afraid to challenge what they are told. Their experience of Sikhism is less cultural and emotional, more intellectual. Culturally, they are more American than they are Indian; in religion, they are Sikh. Frequently, their parents cannot easily communicate the meaning of their own heritage. Then there are the newest arrivals, often the lesser educated Sikhs and relatives who are attracted by the opportunities and by the comforting presence of a community; they want institutions that reflect the cocoon that nurtured and sustained them in India.

The old-world Europeans often look askance at the bold and brassy North American Yankees, and they in turn are disdainful of the Texans who appear to have a special corner on life. To most Indians deeply steeped in culture and tradition, Punjabis seem a lot like the Yankees do to the Europeans, and the Sikhs unquestionably like the Texans — generous, outer-directed, loud, boisterous, somewhat larger than life. At times, there is some scorn and laughter but there is a lot more envy in these perceptions.

Many of our raucous and disagreeable differences reflect the variety in the make up of our community. Also, political events in India, particularly in the last eight years, have left no Sikh unaffected, no matter where he lives. Clearly no single gurdwara or institution can satisfy the needs of such a diverse community. The predictable result is that we capture headlines not for the good we oft might attempt but for our quarrelsome politics and nettlesome personalities; we seem to spin off new gurdwaras by fission and not as a result of coherent or thoughtful planning.

When I look back at the more than three decades that I have spent in this country, it has been a most extraordinary odyssey. When I came here, I was a callow youth. There were only two Sikhs in New York city, many parts of the country had none. The people sat on chairs in the one gurdwara in Stockton, California. I returned to New York ten years later and found perhaps 20 or 30 recognizable Sikhs. We would rent the hall of a church school for a weekly service. The community meal (*langar*) was not possible; tea and cookies were the lubricants of social interaction. I recall when the New York congregation bought a building. The community split over the issue — the building appeared to be so far away and so large. Would we ever have enough people to fill the cavernous hall? Now there are six gurdwaras in the New York metropolitan area. On the holy days, the crowds are so enormous that it seems the buildings are going to come apart at the seams like an egg. As immigration policies relaxed, many more Sikhs sought new lives here. Each generation of Sikhs has paid its dues to this society; we have made a home here with our blood, sweat and tears. We too have carved out a niche for ourselves in the complex mosaic that is America.

When I was one of the few Sikhs in town, it was not uncommon for a church to ask me to come and speak on Sikhism. It is always interesting to see ourselves as others view us. Keep in mind the fact that western interest in eastern religions has rarely extended beyond myth, magic and ritual. I also found out that I knew very little of Sikhism that I could convey in a systematic, organized, formal manner. It seemed that much of what I knew, I had learnt by osmosis.

These essays are an odd collection much as any life is, but in a sense they chronicle how this one individual came to grips with his heritage. They address concerns that have troubled and molded my thinking and my life. Many of my friends will probably take issue with what I say or how I say it, and I hope they do. Sikhs are a vigorous, open people, as is their religion. There should be neither the need nor the expectation of homogeneity of thought or uniformity of opinion. The purpose here is to stir the pot of discussion and debate. Are Sikhs and Sikh institutions ready for the twenty-first century or are they going to be dragged into it kicking and screaming?

Sometimes I think that reason does not govern or direct us very much when we make the most important choices in life, our criteria transcend rational logic. Later, we muster whatever intelligence we have to justify our choices. I am convinced this applies to the facets of our lives that we care the most deeply about — our children, our parents, our friends and our religion.

On Being and
Becoming a Sikh

For over twenty years it has been gnawing at me. Some of us were sitting around discussing for the umpteenth time the politics of our nascent gurdwara in New York. One of us — bright, young, ambitious, highly educated, better read on Sikhism than most of us but unfortunately not a recognizable Sikh — blurted out, "I am just as good a Sikh as any of you, if not better. I have read more about it than perhaps all of you put together." The boast rankled me. Quick as a whip, I lashed out: "Any Sikh who claims to be a *good* Sikh is not." It sounded apt and clever. It certainly hit the mark. Everybody laughed except the poor target. It has been twenty years but he never spoke with me again. Many times I have thought about that day and what it means to be a Sikh.

A farmer dies and his farm goes to his child. A tradesman can leave his shop and a businessman his business, to his progeny. The shop and the profession continue. One can confer an inheritance of millions, even a legacy of generations of Sikh history to one's family. One may bestow truckloads of artifacts, tons of books and libraries of literature on Sikhism. But can one award the spirit of Sikhism to one's children?

There are families which have for generations treasured handwritten letters and documents by Guru Nanak, Guru Gobind Singh or others close to the Gurus. There are many who claim to be descended from one Guru or another. There are the so called scions of the Gurus who travel around India from village to village collecting donations from gullible Sikhs who feel honored by the touch of the son of a son of a son of a son of a Guru. Can that make them good Sikhs? Can one will the grant of Sikhism?

Isn't it best, as Abraham Lincoln is reputed to have said, to be less anxious about who your grandfather was and more concerned with what his grandson is up to? If the sons of Guru Gobind Singh were brimming with the spirit of Sikhism, it was not because they were the sons of a Guru. Other sons of other Gurus have found no place in our hearts or in our history. Where others had failed, the sons of the tenth Guru had assimilated the lessons of Sikhism. They had earned Sikhism, not inherited it. The sons of Guru Gobind Singh are remembered every day in our prayers not because they were sons of a Guru but because they had worked their way into the marrow of our collective consciousness. Many other sons of other Gurus were quickly forgotten and merited unmarked graves.

It is true that you cannot take the material things of life with you; you can bequeath them to your descendants, friends or a worthier cause. If you don't, the government might steal a chunk. But it is also true that you cannot donate to anybody else the spirit of Sikhism that you have integrated within yourself. One cannot inherit Sikhism for that is not how Sikhs are made. One can be born in a Sikh household. One can acquire the Sikh uniform. One can even learn the protocol, formality and etiquette of the religion. All that does not make a Sikh. The rituals that one masters remain exactly that — rituals; the uniform, a disguise or an empty shell. Only the individual prayer and the Guru's grace may transform them into sacraments, and the best prayer is honest self-effort.

By teaching, by example and through the *Guru Granth*, the Gurus have shown the student Sikh how best to direct his individual efforts. But each person has to discover the path by and for himself. This voyage of discovery is an inner journey and a lovely one which every pilgrim must undertake on his own.

The lives of the Gurus and the teachings of the *Guru Granth* provide a map only. The map has to be read and the path chalked by each traveler himself. And for the pilgrim who sets foot on the seemingly lonely path honestly and boldly, the Guru promises to show the way and provide the finest company.

It is no coincidence that the religion is called Sikhism and the followers Sikhs — literally, students. It is a constant reminder that the Sikh, to be true to his label, cannot afford to be anything but a student all his life. He or she remains a student of the way of life as enunciated by the Gurus. Quite simply then, the emphasis shifts from being a Sikh to the developmental direction of becoming one. And the continuous, ongoing, life-long, active process of metamorphosis — internal change — becomes the focus.

Concomitantly, one also becomes aware that Sikhism is not now a static or dormant discipline nor was it ever. For the two hundred years from Guru Nanak to Guru Gobind Singh, it remained in a state of continuous flux and development. Now three hundred years after Guru Gobind Singh, Sikhism continues to grow and wrestle with new issues that engage it — from ecology, peace and disarmament, gender and racial discrimination to the population explosion, reproductive rights and AIDS — matters that affect us all. Not that Sikhism ever does or should take clear, unvarying positions on many of these matters, but it provides the Sikh a highly developed, structured sense of ethics so that individually or collectively, he can make responsible choices in all things. Sikhism acknowledges that many of the judgments that we make today on these and other issues might change in time and with individual circumstances and greater social or scientific awareness.

What does it mean to be a *good* Sikh? An excellent student is one who has never yet failed an examination. But that record of success speaks only of the past, the future is yet to be. Even the best student will falter, and fail a test — sometimes. The glory lies not in never falling but in rising every time one falls. It is a never ending process. There are many stages in all aspects of one's development — be it physical, mental, psychological, spiritual or even financial. Life shows many milestones in its path; they are like the rites of passage. In one's professional growth, a diploma is hardly the end of learning and growing. In reality it marks only the beginning of a life-long career, a commitment in which one continues to develop as one practices the profession over the years. A true professional can ill afford to be anything but a student all his life.

By this reasoning, even the rite of confirmation in the Sikh religion (*Amrit*) becomes a rite of passage, an important rung in that ladder and a stage in the developmental process of becoming a Sikh. For a confirmed (*Amritdhari*) Sikh to become haughty or smug of his status or self-satisfied and vain of his dedication would be unbecoming. He has reached a recognizable, enviable and honorable rung on the ladder, but the ladder is tall and its end nowhere in sight. While we can commend him for his effort and progress, a little feeling for the path yet untravelled would be more seemly on his part. A sense of gratitude to God from whom all things flow coupled with a little humility is necessary, for anyone might slip.

In essence, every Sikh is a convert to the religion, being born into it merely gives one a head start on the rules and the layout of the track, if one so chooses; it does not automatically make one into a winner. Being a Sikh is often only an accident of birth; the developmental process of becoming a Sikh is indeed much more significant. Sikhs are not born but made.

The Sikhs and
their Guru

The Sikh religion is unusual in many ways, not the least of those
is the unique relationship of the Sikhs to their Guru. A sacred
bond exists between the Sikh and the Guru. The light of God
burns in all though in most of us it is considerably dimmed by
the desperation of our lives. In the Guru, that light is bright as
the sun which can give life to many if only they are willing. Yet,
the Sikh does not worship the Guru — Nanak or Gobind Singh.
Worship only the immaculate, infinite one who is never born
and never dies and is subject to no human calculations or
formulations, so said the Sikh Gurus. For two hundred years,
the spark lit by Guru Nanak was fanned and more kindling was
added until it was a roaring fire of a spiritual revolution. Guru
Gobind Singh then baptized the first five Sikhs. But then he
knelt before them so that they could in turn baptize him. In a
sense, he elevated them to his own level. Yet a Sikh remains
forever a 'sikh' — a pupil, a learner — at the feet of his Guru.

When the time came for Guru Gobind Singh to anoint a
successor, he recognized that his followers had come a long way
along the path of self-realization from the time when Guru
Nanak first ignited the spark. He established, therefore, the
Guru Granth as the repository of all spiritual authority. He also
understood that many of the problems of daily living that
people will face are time-bound or culture-based and will have
to be decided by people according to the needs of the times, but
consistent with their history, spiritual heritage and tradition.
Therefore, he vested his Sikhs with all temporal authority. The

mystical presence of the Guru, therefore, manifests in the congregation in mindful prayer (*Sangat*) and the Guru speaks to us through the *Guru Granth* ; the operational words here are "mindful prayer." When the aura is such that the joy of love, devotion and commitment meld the Sikh to the word of the *Guru Granth*, then no disparity remains between the Sikh and his Guru.

In many ways, the *Guru Granth* is like a book of recipes or prescriptions. Just reading such a book is not going to assuage the hunger or cure any ailment. To savor the delights of the food, one would have to labor and prepare it first. The recipes in the *Guru Granth* can be a panacea for one's soul only if they are formulated and internalized. The *Guru* in the *granth* comes alive only when the reader imbibes and assimilates the message that he recites. For a Sikh, the *Guru Granth* is a book to be read, pondered and absorbed, yet it is more than that. The whole relationship of the Sikh to the *Guru Granth* serves to integrate the man of action with his spiritual self, so that in every moment of life and in everything he does, he acts with an awareness of the infinite within him. Our senses cannot perceive him, and our intellect cannot plumb his depths, yet our souls can commune with him. Yet, when I say "Him" or "He" or in another turn of the phrase refer to God as 'She' or "Her," the limitations of the English language and the paucity of the human imagination and experience become apparent ; they force me to describe and define a lesser, partisan "god." Many times and in many places in the Sikh scriptures, God is defined as free of form, race, caste or gender. As the repository of all spiritual authority, to the Sikh the *Guru Granth* becomes more than just another "holy book." In that sense, it is not like the *Torah*, the *Bible* or the *Koran*.

With this prelude, it is easy to understand the ceremonies and rituals that serve to define the relationship between a Sikh and *Guru Granth*. A Sikh starts and ends every day by appearing before his Guru. He does so by going to a meditation room in his house or a gurdwara or by spending a moment in meditation by himself or with family. A reading from the *Guru Granth* becomes a command to guide his day—a day to be spent in honest labor, love and sacrifice. A Sikh appears before his Guru as if in the court of the mightiest monarch, the creator of us all — with humility, prayer and confidence. The rules of behavior become simple and depend upon history, culture and common sense, not canon.

The room for the *Guru Granth* should be clean and free of negative vibrations. Drugs, alcohol, tobacco or other intoxicants are not admissible. The devotee appears without shoes and with covered head. Non-spiritual, secular matters are best left outside that room. The canopy, the vestments and other accoutrements of the *Guru Granth* need not be elaborate or extravagant. They need only be clean, consistent with one's economic resources and reflective of one's devotion. The best devotion would be such reverence for the word of the Guru that it becomes integrated into one's life. Temples to God can remain God-like only if they stay simple in keeping with the resources of the people, else they become monuments to the ego of the builders. Only a lesser god would have very elaborate needs and he or she would not be deserving of worship.

The atmosphere surrounding the *Guru Granth* should be such that it compels one to immerse oneself in the word and presence of God. Extraneous conversation and activity would be a distraction. Monetary or other offerings should be presented with devotion and not thrown as if at a beggar. One must give one's soul before one's money finds acceptance in the house of the Guru. In a gurdwara needless interruptions, whether to announce lists of donors or to comment on events or programs are unwelcome. In short, whatever robs the atmosphere of a spirituality in which one can lose oneself is unacceptable, whatever enhances that aura is desirable. The

Guru Granth speaks of this aura as such that one becomes attuned to vibrations of the divine music within the self.

Appearance before the Guru can be likened to a retreat. It should prepare and allow one to venture forth into the secular world with spirits high, a mind at peace and a heart full of love and joy. Every time, therefore, that we appear before the Guru, we renew ourselves. The ambiance and the worship must be such as to transform the galloping restless mind so that it can, if only for a trice, become one with the infinite; where traditions, history and human hopes merge; where the past, present and future come together in an endless moment.

The Man for all Seasons

The Sikhs have some remarkably different and contradictory ways of looking at their Gurus. Their religion says that God is free from the cycle of human birth, hence is never born nor dies. We also believe that God speaks to us through the Gurus and their teaching. What then of the divinity of the Gurus from Nanak to Gobind Singh? If Jesus was the son of God, how about Guru Nanak or Guru Gobind Singh? For that matter, how about you and I? When Guru Arjan and Guru Tegh Bahadur were martyred, did they feel the pain? Did Guru Gobind Singh suffer the loneliness of war and desertion, and the anguish of every parent when he lost his sons in battle?

These and other questions were brought home to me two or three years back. I had been asked to formulate a series of questions based on a book on Guru Gobind Singh for a discussion group. One general question asked: "What kind of a man was he?" Some Sikhs who had a preview of the questionnaire took offence. Guru Gobind Singh, they insisted, should not be referred to as a man for he was divine. My words were blasphemy to them. I hid behind a verse of Bhai Nandlal, a poet who knew and traveled with Guru Gobind Singh and referred affectionately and reverently to the Guru as "A man -nonpareil."

We recognize at a certain level of awareness that men like Jesus, Nanak, Gobind Singh were special - beyond human understanding - so much so that we unnecessarily free them of all human experiences, particularly those that are universally recognized as painful or noxious. The epitome of such reasoning is seen in Christianity, where in order to emphasize the uniqueness of Christ, theologians have recast his birth and death in terms which deny him his humanity. To be virgin-born is not human, nor is it to be raised from the dead. The claim of virgin birth is not unique to Christianity; it is found much earlier in Egyptian mythology and in the life of Buddha as well. Similar reasoning is encountered when Christ is viewed as the only son of God, begotten not made like you or I. If God does not assume human forms, such claims cannot be taken literally. It seems to me that as sons or daughters of God you and I are no less, the difference between Christ and us may lie in the inadequacy of our lives and surely it is a quantum difference. In Guru Gobind Singh's words, God said to him: "I ordain you as my son. Go forth ....." Such words in Christianity and in Sikhism need to be interpreted with some sensitivity and intelligence not transliterated. In very blunt language, Gobind Singh also directed his followers not to worship him as God.

Such claims as we make on behalf of our prophets and seers are merely indicative of our own very human inadequacies and insecurities. These claims are unnecessary, and to dismiss them would not diminish any great men of God. The uniqueness of Christ, Buddha, Nanak or Gobind Singh lies in how they lived and what they taught, not in how or where they were born or what happened to them after they died.

If at martyrdom Guru Arjan and Tegh Bahadur felt no pain then they did not suffer. If they did not suffer as we lesser mortals do, what can they tell us about human suffering? How can they show us the way? Christ was not without suffering when he wailed: "Father, why have thou forsaken me?" When Guru Arjan was tortured 1600 years later, he felt the pain though he did not lament his suffering. God the Father had not abandoned him. Instead, Guru Arjan essentially said: "Thy will be done." His words at that time were of cheerful acceptance of the will of God and the wish always to be imbued with the love of God. Guru Gobind Singh saw his two young teenaged sons go to war, never to return. He knew when his two younger sons were bricked up alive but did not recant their faith. His answer speaks of the man: "What if I have lost four sons, there are countless more." He was pointing to his followers then. Surely, he knew a father's pain. Certainly, the Gurus shared our human experience but were able to transcend it. Otherwise, they would have little to show us and nothing to teach us. If they felt no pain, what can they tell us about it? If they faced no temptation, they can hardly teach us how to manage ours.

On the other hand, I look at the political divisions and factions in our young Sikh community. I have come to see how difficult it is to knit our vibrant Sikhs into a unified group and lead them towards a common goal in a single direction. The Gurus created a pride of lions, not a flock of sheep - a nation of individuals, fearless and not afraid to go alone. Yet, these same Sikhs who follow no man, willingly and freely followed their Gurus through pain, suffering, war and often to certain death; and now hundreds of years later, in the name of their Gurus, they still walk that road and the extra mile. I wonder if there can be a more vivid proof of the Gurus' divinity. I think, in fruitless arguments about the humanity or divinity of the Gurus, we miss or devalue the essential elements of their teaching.

The core of Sikh teaching - how to live and die with dignity -had to be taught by example. Mere words would lose relevance with time. The Gurus taught that salvation does not lie in renunciation but in a life of involvement as a householder. Marry, have a family, make an honest living, share the rewards of life with your fellow beings, and spend a life with your mind attuned to the infinite reality within. In a life devoted to truth, be prepared to lay your life on the line for honesty, integrity and honor. These are the essentials of a useful, productive life.

The Gurus taught that empowerment of a people occurs only when they have learned the essentials of a good, centered life where God is sought through a responsible, ethical life of honest self-effort and service to mankind. The inner life must be consistent with and effortlessly merged with the external reality of action in the society and this world. Worship no one but the infinite within, serve no master but truth, live a productive life within the community, taught the Gurus. Truth and truthful living were the first lessons of Sikhism that Guru Nanak gave. He taught the way to responsible, ethical, honest family life. By example and by teaching, the Gurus rejected the caste system, elevated women to equal status, taught people to share, and so on.

The Gurus lived at a time and in a society where life and liberty of a non-Muslim were not safe. Practices such as the caste-system, female infanticide and *suttee* dominated Hinduism. A multi-dimensional struggle for a just society was necessary. However, much as one does not entrust a bankbook to a child or a car to one who cannot drive, Nanak did not ask his followers to take up arms against tyranny and injustice. The followers had to develop the maturity, judgement, and discipline for that. Before you pick up a weapon you must know what it is to die. Before you acquire power you must learn what it is to be powerless, lest you become a despot. To command one must learn to serve. Each Guru added a chapter to this book of lessons started by Nanak; each lesson added another dimension to the Sikh - the new man, a man for all seasons.

But it is one thing to preach and quite another to do. The Gurus therefore, lived what they taught. Now as long as Sikhs remember their history, they will retain the lessons.

The Gurus had shown what it is to lead a life of service. Guru Arjan and Tegh Bahadur had shown how to die with dignity for a principle. Guru Hargobind and Gobind Singh could now ask this new man - the mature Sikh - to maintain weapons but use them only if absolutely necessary for justice. By the time that the Sikh was given the power of a giant, he had learned not to use it like one. Guru Gobind Singh's life was a demonstration-lesson on what it is to be completely human and a complete man in all of human dimensions - a man for all seasons.

Not so long ago when my hundredth research publication appeared in print, I felt proud as a peacock. To me and my friends it was quite a landmark. But what is the measure of a man? Guru Gobind Singh showed a different yardstick. He lived the family life, married and had children. His children turned out well for none betrayed him but lived a life of rectitude, nobility, character and bravery. What more can a father ask? Guru Gobind Singh was an accomplished soldier and a General. He created a productive, fearless and honest nation out of powerless people at the fringes of society. He created leaders out of ordinary men and then subjected himself to the will of his followers. He created a nation and then credited his followers for all that he had accomplished. His door was open to the powerless as well as the elite of the day. What greater administrative skills and dedication to the public good can one have? He was a philosopher, a writer, a poet extraordinaire. To pen over a thousand pages of verse in a variety of languages is no mean achievement. To dictate the whole *Guru Granth* - all 1430 pages - from memory is no ordinary skill. A connoisseur of the arts, 52 poets and many musicians sought his patronage. Guru Gobind Singh's life illustrated all the dimensions of the human existence. And he lived for only 42 years - an age at which many of us are still finding ourselves. Where most of us once dead are soon forgotten, three hundred years after Guru Gobind Singh people argue about whether he was divine. Now that is a yardstick for the measure of a man.

The concept of original sin is not found in Sikhism, nor the idea that woman is conceived any differently - from Adam's rib, for instance - or is any less. In the Sikh view human birth is special for in the human condition man can aspire to be divine. Sikhism is a religion of joy, not of sin. Human birth is not a fall from grace but not to fulfill its potential and its destiny would be. Knowledge is not sin, its abuse and misuse would be sinful. The sin is not in being human but in not becoming all we can be as humans.

"Man is a useless passion" Sartre claimed. Sikhism would passionately disagree. Sikhism holds for a state of impermeable equanimity like that achieved by a candle in a windless place, where one is in tune with the vibrations of divine music - suffused by bliss, undiminished by joy or sorrow, loss or gain, unaffected by the slings and arrows of outrageous fortune. The ultimate measure of one's divinity lies in one's humanity. To be completely human by developing all that is human and noble is to become divine. That is the only divinity, the only eternity, the only immortality open to man. To be more is not possible, to be any less is not to be fully human but to remain incomplete.

The Roots of Sikhism

I think it was the historian Toynbee who said that the Vedantic and Judaic disciplines — the two great religious systems of the world — met in northern India. Collided would be more like it. Their confrontation spawned a new order — Sikhism — which has some elements of each but in other matters, rejects both. Toynbee saw in Sikhism a synthesis of the best of the two noble religious systems. Many Sikhs look at their religion not as a philosophy of synthesis but as a new, revealed religion with little debt to the existing traditions.

Clearly, religions or any philosophic systems for that matter do not arise in a vacuum. A novel, fresh way of living must reflect on the old even if only to reject it but in that process becomes influenced by what is rejected. Therefore in most beliefs and practices, a pattern of continuity between the old and the new is never very difficult to discern. That is no proof that the new is merely a revamping and repackaging of the old, nor that it is a new superstructure constructed entirely or primarily on the old substructure. Some historians spend lifetimes counting bricks to see which ones or how many in the foundation of Sikhism are from the old edifice, others expend their energy denying *in toto* the existence of any old masonry in the new institution.

Even the most radical new design must derive in some part from the pre-existing one even though in some fundamentally new ways. All new life emerges from the old and revolutions do not occur in a void. In the final analysis, the proof of how new is new rests with how revolutionized, changed, charged or new

24

do the believers feel. If both Hindus and Muslims lay claim to some features of Sikhism (as they do), that is a compliment to the Sikhs and their dynamic, young religion. Nobody wants to assert a kinship with one not admired. And such contentions do not detract from the revolutionary or the revealed nature of Sikhism though many Sikhs would like to disavow any connection to the old roots, whether Semitic or Hindu Vedantic.

Like the semitic religions — Judaism, Christianity and Islam □ Sikhism is a religion of the Book; Hinduism is not. Where Hinduism has a virtual army of gods and goddesses, Sikhism is like Judaism — strictly monotheistic. The Judaic God is an immanent God and an angry, wrathful, revengeful one. With Christianity came a transformation and humanization of this God into a loving, forgiving father image. Because of the plethora of gods and goddesses, the Hindu God is not so easily defined but is probably transcendental in nature. The Sikh concept of God is one who is both immanent and transcendental, righteously just but also merciful. Where theologians and their ilk love to write treatises, this very short treatment will have to suffice even though it is equally unjust to the Judaic, Hindu or Sikh views of God.

Part of the problem in our understanding lies in the fact that both Judaism and Hinduism are ancient systems with their origins lost in antiquity. When it comes to Hinduism the historical record is even murkier. The old, diffuse religions of mythology prevailed not only in Greece, Norway, Rome or Egypt but similar conceptualizations were also the underpinning of ancient Indian civilization. To me, many of the gods and goddesses of Hinduism are not so different from the heroic and some not so noble figures of Greek mythology, and should be similarly interpreted. Certainly the stories about Echo, Narcissus, Hercules, Aphrodite, etc. in Greek mythology have no literal reality. The stories in Hindu mythology about Brahma, Indra, Shiva, Durga, Lakshmi, beginning of the world, even the

Ramayana and the *Bhagvad Gita* are apocryphal and not meant to be literally understood. In spite of India's astronomical population, there are perhaps more gods and goddesses in Hindu mythology than people.

In Europe, however, a new religion with a defined theology — Christianity — unrelated to the native mythology and independent of it in origin took hold and supplanted it. Pre-Christian mythology surely influenced many Christian beliefs and practices but it is easy to see that the two — Greek mythology and Christianity — are distinct entities and remain so. Mythology served its purposes in helping early man define his place in the universe. Later, the organized religion of Christianity provided a clearer ethical framework, a more sophisticated system for defining the nature of man and his inner reality in relation to society. In Hinduism, however, a radically different kind of development occurred. The Vedantic system was superimposed on the existing mythology but did not displace and replace it. Instead, the religion of mythology became overlaid with a patina of highly sophisticated Vedantic philosophy; the two become so inseparable that Hinduism came to be defined through mythology. Mythology and philosophy became so enmeshed in the common mind and daily practice that it became well nigh impossible to identify the individual strands. That remains true even today.

At least two major religions — Buddhism and Sikhism — devoid of mythological baggage did originate in India. Buddhism has been pretty much lost to its native soil although it is widely extant in many neighboring countries. Sikhism has endured because of its discrete theology, its proven ability to fight for survival and its distinct symbols. Though under constant assault, it may even be at the threshold of a renaissance at this time.

Hinduism contends that God has taken human birth nine times and will once again, sometime in the future. Christianity presents passionate arguments for Christ as the son of God — begotten not made. The preamble to Sikhism defines God as one who is free of birth and death.   Worship only the one Immaculate, all-pervasive Creator, not the Gurus and not any holy book, say the Sikh Gurus. And we are all sons and daughters of God. God is to be found neither on a mountaintop by a recluse nor by the celibate clergyman in the service of the Church. Marry, have a family and live a productive life of honest earnings and share what you have, keeping your mind attuned to the infinite within you. God the creator is revealed through his creation, not to live in harmony with it is a sin. Ritual animal sacrifice is, therefore, not right though Sikhs are not vegetarians by any religious law. In referring to God as the male father figure, we are limited by the paucity of language and thought in expressing ideas. God in the Sikh view has no gender, race, lineage or form; He is free of all physical attributes that man can conceive. Sikhs refer to God as father, mother, brother, sister and friend. A god who is a he or she is a lesser god not worthy of worship.

God is to be remembered not for an hour in a temple or a church on a Sunday but must become an integral, internalized part of one's life, one who is never forgotten even for a moment. By analogies from farming— "The body is the soil, good deeds the plough," from trading or from ordinary habits of simple people — "Make truth your prayer, faith your prayer mat", the message of Sikhism was simple yet direct: Truth is high, higher yet is truthful living.   Therefore, Sikhs do not speak of a sabbath, a holy day of atonement or remembrance, nor do they ascribe special significance to any day of the week or month or any hour of the day. Any chore no matter how mundane, performed with an awareness of the Infinite within is sacred; even the most sacred task accomplished without that perception is profane. Similarly a day, an hour, even a moment spent in God's grace is sacred, else it's wasted.   One cannot buy indulgences from God by asking a holy man to perform prayers, rituals or ceremonies on one's behalf, no matter how pious the priest or how expensive the ceremony.

A literal interpretation of mythology can be risky and Guru Nanak offered a surprisingly modern view of creation when he spoke of the void before creation, and of many galaxies and universes—without end and innumerable. He clearly refuted as nonsense any claims to knowing exactly what hour, day or year the world began or when it would end.

Perhaps the most visible point of divergence of Sikhism from Judaic philosophy lies in the concept of original sin which is not found in the Sikh view. Sikhs believe that human life is special — a rare opportunity to serve both man and God. The human body is the mansion of God, a temple to be maintained well and healthy. There is no room for mortification of the flesh, whether by fasting or otherwise. The sin lies not in living comfortably or well but in not using one's blessings in service to others, for that is the way to find God. To leave the world a little better is a duty; not to try, a sin. Sikhism asserts that the kingdom of heaven is open to all irrespective of caste, creed, sex or ethnic origin. Sexism and racism of any sort thus become failures in the practice of Sikh teaching. Those who are at one with God and Guru are the chosen people, not those of any particular caste, creed or ethnicity. Between man and God no middlemen exist, no brokers are necessary. This also means that the authority and the role of the clergy are limited — defined by the scholarship and the persona of the man, not by canon.

In biology, hybridization is known to produce a more spirited stock. This is true of horses as it is of people and I suspect, equally valid for philosophies. Whether it was the Aryans from the Caucasus, the hordes of Alexander the Great or the innumerable invasions through the Khyber Pass, Punjab was the fertile field for such mixtures of both people and ideas. The

Punjabi stock, therefore, turned out more vigorous, energetic and outgoing. So is their new ideology of Sikhism — a religion of joy, not suffering. When Christianity was young, many Jews accepted Jesus as the promised Messiah but remained Jews — for Jesus. Now 2,000 years later, the movement is not as strong but still exists. Sikhism is only 500 years old and if you count from the time that Guru Gobind Śingh gave it the present form, about 300 years young. Three centuries are barely a drop in the bucket of human history. It is hardly surprising that some followers have one leg in the boat of Hinduism and the other in Sikhism. There are many Hindus who never formally accepted Sikhism — Sindhis, for instance — yet the only scriptures they read are Sikh, the only house of worship they know is Sikh. Others attend both Hindu and Sikh or Muslim and Sikh services. Christianized Muslims (Morisos) of Africa come to mind as a parallel.

Almost from their inception, Sikhs have had to fight and die for their religion. It is no wonder that some followers practised Sikhism at home but remained most reluctant to be so identified publicly. Under similar duress, the Marrano Jews remained Jews at home but outside, adopted the rituals and the lifestyles of Christians. One intriguing historical curiosity that I often saw as a child is worth noting. Since Sikhs were always fighting for survival, many Punjabi Hindu families would dedicate one son to Sikhism. By making one child a Sikh, they acknowledged their debt to and respect for the Sikh way of life, while at the same time they confessed the inability of the entire family to walk that perilous path.

If Sikhism brought the idea of eventual justice — *Karma* — from Hinduism, it freed the doctrine of its overtones of sexism and shackles of the caste system. Curiously, Islam found no place for music in worship; Hinduism on the other hand, not only exalted the development of music to a fine art but even mandated dancing girls and vestal virgins. Sikhism, like Christianity, recognized the ability of music to move people to a spiritual high minus, of course, the dancing girls. In Hinduism congregational worship is unimportant; much more significant — even to the exclusion of everything else — is private meditation. Judaism with its two children — Christianity and Islam — emphasized much more the social aspect of man's obligation and congregational worship became supreme. Sikhism recognizes the worth of both. Private meditation is important for it allows man to discover the truth within. Congregational worship is necessary for it defines man in terms of the universe outside of him. In the Sikh view, the mystical presence of God pervades a congregation in mindful prayer; such a congregation remains in Sikh doctrine the supreme source of all temporal authority.

The essence of a Sikh life could be summarized as having three important aspects, like the legs of a stable stool: a life of honest work, honestly spent; sharing the rewards of such a life with fellow men; and both of those activities to be accomplished with a mind centered on the infinite within. Nobody would deny the worth of the first two commandments, many such as the prominent writer Khushwant Singh fail to acknowledge that if man were more cognizant of the Infinite within, he would be more aware of his place within the creation and more in tune with the fundamental unity of all of God's creation. All creation, human and otherwise, would then be less subject to man's puffed up sense of self. That third leg of the stool, an essential element of Sikh teaching, allows Man to look beyond the self at human life as a rare opportunity to enrich his environment including his fellow creatures.

There are other ways in which Sikhism departs from both the Judaic and Hindu traditions and which stem from the enhanced place of the lay follower in Sikhism. For instance, the concept seen in Christianity of the clergy as shepherds leading a flock, or the primary role of the Brahmin as the essential middleman are anathema to Sikhs. Since a middleman or broker is not recognized, the power and authority of the clergy is necessarily curtailed. The scriptures are available to all — laity or clergy, men or women, high of birth or otherwise. Parenthetically, I should add that Hindu scriptures are not available to the lower castes and may not be read by women. Also, the Council of Narbonne in 1229 forbade the possession of any part of the Bible by laymen; this was not corrected until centuries later. In Sikhism, no one may deny another the right to attend or perform any aspect of any Sikh service and it need not be only in a gurdwara but can be anywhere, even a house; no approval from any clergy for any religious service is necessary. It is worth noting that, because Sikhism is so young, the compilation, authenticity and authorship of the Sikh scriptures are clearly and simply established. Such a claim is not easily made by many of the older religious systems.

It seems to me that when man finds himself in conflict with his environment as he inevitably must, the Judeo-Christian and the Hindu-Vedantic traditions provide him diametrically opposite ways of dealing with it. The primarily western Judeo-Christian outlook exemplified by the North-American lifestyle says: "The world is not as it should be and I am going to change the outer reality to be consonant with what I want it to be. I am going to master nature, recast it into my own view and make a difference even if I die trying." Frequently both things happen. Technological revolutions are unleashed, and we change the world around us to what we want it to be. But the price we pay is spiritual, and horrendous. Just look at the disintegration of the individual, dissolution of the family and collapse of society; otherwise our psychiatrists and lawyers would not be so busy. On the other hand, in a similar conflict with the environment, the Asian approach epitomized by the Hindu-Vedantic attitude is dramatically different. It says in effect: "The external world is not as it should be. But there is

a universe within the self which is infinite and far more
beautiful. I am going to close my eyes, turn inward and be at
peace." The desired result is achieved but at what cost? One
can exist for 2000 years in filth, amidst injustice, yet the mind
is at peace and all is right with the world. Progress can become
unnecessary, if not impossible or undesirable.

Clearly, both attitudes are wanting. Sikhism directs that one
be at peace within and at the same time be externally directed
so as to make a difference. Vedantic Hinduism regards the body
as a prison for the soul, this results in a curious unworldliness or
other worldliness in Hinduism. Sikhism regards the body as the
temple of God who is to be discovered by serving and living
with fellow humans. Hindu mythology would tell us this world
is unreal, a dream, not a tangible reality — Sikhism would agree
only so that one may remain detached from this world, and as
long as one remembers that this world is also true and it is by
truthful living in this world that one will find the God within
each of us. Be like the lotus that may exist in a cesspool yet
remains unblemished but serves others by its fragrance.

Tradition or Habits of the Heart

Sometimes I think that the dead rule the living through tradition. The reverence shown by most people for tradition is misplaced and only serves to spare the living the inconvenience of having to do their own thinking. By hiding behind tradition, we shift responsibility on the dead who cannot answer. By wrapping tradition in an aura of holiness, we create guilt in the living for even daring to question it. Something does not become good merely because it is new, nor because it has been around for years. What is wheat and what is chaff in what we call tradition?

Are we prisoners of culture and tradition? The traditional Hindu adores the past and prays for a future but does he sleepwalk through the present? Is he bound to what was? The existentialist has no use for the past and little hope for the future; he only knows the present. To him the past is dead and buried, the future yet unborn. He is alive to the present but doesn't he have an incomplete view of existence and reality? Is he whole? Are there any uses to the past? With time, the pristine practices of the past acquire more weight, grow more cumbersome, stifling and meaningless. How to separate what is real from what is dross?

Hardly a day goes by when in some gurdwara someone doesn't declaim: "One does not become a Sikh just by growing one's hair; a revolution in one's lifestyle is necessary." There is hardly any Sikh tradition or practice that has not been challenged by Sikh theologians. Yet, none but Sikhs could be more scornful of another Sikh who rejects or is ignorant of Sikh

33

tradition. The first attitude of not giving blind obedience to tradition springs from Sikh teaching. It is reminiscent of Guru Nanak and Guru Gobind Singh who questioned Hindu and Muslim practices forthrightly and boldly set on to shatter the existing order, whether it pertained to the place of women, idol worship or the caste system. The daily prayer of the Sikhs also includes one plea: the boon of mental acuity and the skill of critical thinking. How then could a Sikh be anything but an iconoclast? How could he give unquestioning loyalty to tradition? The second attitude of reverence for tradition comes from a subconscious understanding of the uses of the past and from the sure knowledge that given their checkered history, without awareness of tradition, Sikhs would revert and collapse into the predominant society around them — in India Hinduism would surely absorb them.

The past has its uses. It is not just a chain that we carry with us and that holds us back. It is not just a burden to be lugged around. If it is chain, it is loose enough to permit us much free will, yet strong enough to bind us to reality; without it, we might lose all sense of self, and like an untethered hot-air balloon disappear into the sunset. The past is a prologue to the future.

About 15 years ago, Alex Haley's book *Roots* hit like a bombshell. For Black Americans, encountering *Roots* was the most liberating event since the Civil War or the 1965 march in Selma, Alabama. An overstatement? Yes. But the importance of *Roots* to contemporary Black consciousness cannot be ignored. And this was a book hardly noticed for much literary merit. For many Blacks, the book was a logical sequel to the 'Black is Beautiful' movement of the 1960s. A sense of identity and self-worth are inseparable and indispensable to a life of dignity. One must know where one is coming from and *Roots* spurred that process for the Black Americans. That message of *Roots* was crystallized in an episode where Kizzy talking of Sam says: "Nobody ever told him where he came from. So he didn't have a dream of where he ought to be going." The Holocaust cruelly but surely brought that point home to most Jews.

A pervasive sense of rootlessness is as American as apple pie. We who come here from elsewhere experience it as we encounter the cultural shock of a wholly different, somewhat alien environment. Our reactions are understandably visceral and not necessarily rational. Either we retreat into a shell and a cultural ghetto of the mind ensues, or we chose anonymity in the crowd. The preferred alternative is to raise our consciousness to the level where identity and integration do not remain mutually exclusive, but complement each other like the components of a mosaic — where the whole becomes larger than the sum of the parts. A people who are not at peace with their past cannot face their future with any degree of faith and hope, and that is the most important message of *Roots*.

Traditions change or die only after a historical catastrophe which greatly alters a people's perception of self and their destiny. Traditions cannot be invented at will or intentionally produced by committees like advertising jingles. These habits of the heart grow out of the collective consciousness of a people and have to be accepted by the subconscious dimension of their being. Man's cultural history is expressed through traditions, whose power does not emanate from any utilitarian value they might possess.

Tradition is often defined through symbols. I shall deal elsewhere with many of the visible ones of Sikhism; here I want to talk generally about the uses and abuses of traditions and to stir up a debate about some common long-standing Sikh practices. Why do Sikhs bow so deeply to the *Guru Granth*? What is this money that they place at the altar in front of the holy book? Why do they usually accept *parshad* only in cupped bare hands and not in a plate? Why do they cover their heads and take off their shoes when they enter the gurdwara? Why is there a canopy above the *Guru Granth*? And a flywhisk? Why is the holy book wrapped up so exquisitely in fancy coverings? What are the traditional functions of a gurdwara and how can they change? Why are Sikhs so deeply attached to the Punjabi language in *Gurmukhi* script? And on and on!

Religion, culture and language are inseparably intertwined; language being the most important repository of a heritage. Without a living language, a people can neither preserve nor transmit, or bring to life a way of thinking and being. Coleridge was correct in saying: "Language is the armory of the human mind and bears within itself, the trophies of the past and the weapons of its future conquests." The death of existing symbols and language constitutes cataclysmic events no less important than the phenomena that generate them and give them birth. Notice the number of radio, newspaper and television advertisements that exhort Jews to learn Hebrew and Jewish history, and further tell them where they can do so at nominal cost.

Guru Gobind Singh was indeed farsighted. He saw that in time many worldly matters will affect the Sikhs, for which a mature community should be able to find answers after careful deliberation. For such issues which are bound by time and culture, he provided the Sikhs a framework for reflection — meetings to be held by the community with the presence and the authority of the *Guru Granth* providing a spiritual focus. Hence every Sikh function—be it birth, death, marriage or the construction of a political agenda requires the presence of the *Guru Granth* and a congregation in mindful prayer.

A Sikh approaches the *Guru Granth* with an attitude of complete surrender. With such reverence to the *Guru Granth*, it is not surprising that the Sikh comes to the Guru with his head covered, as a barefoot penitent, and touches his head to the ground. One does not appear before a mighty monarch empty-handed, and nor does a Sikh appear thus before his Guru. At one time in history, Sikhs offered horses, grain, sugar, fruits or whatever gift they could muster or however the spirit moved them. From these gifts, the Guru would help the needy, run a free kitchen, propagate religion or equip an army. Times and circumstances have changed. Cash offering is more convenient to both the giver and the gurdwara, who can plan more effectively how they want to spend it in the Guru's work. The tradition of tithing is still alive in many Sikh families. The Sikh receives *parshad* as a benediction from the house of the Guru with humility — exemplified by cupped hands and a prayer of thanks. The canopy and the flywhisk are time-honored reminders of the symbols of royalty. I was astonished to learn that sometimes the building of the Golden Temple is washed with milk; such a practice is routine in most Hindu temples. I think the milk belongs in babies where it would do more good, the buildings would be cleaner using soap and water and more sanctified by a congregation united in mindful prayer.

The *Guru Granth* is the Guru but is also a book. The Guru comes alive only when the book is read and absorbed. In the pre-printing press days, only handwritten copies were available. In a village, where one could count on the fingers of one's hand the number of people who could write, copies of the *Guru Granth* were at a premium. A volume of over 1,400 pages was not easy to transcribe. Is it any wonder that whoever had a copy guarded it and treasured it most reverently? It was also the Guru. So the book received the best care, and was wrapped in silks. So much so that many Sikhs were outraged when the first copies were printed; they were fearful that during printing or later, the holy book would not receive the reverence that the Guru and a rare manuscript deserved.

A gurdwara or a Sikh Center should certainly inform us on all aspects of our life in North America or wherever else we live, but it should also provoke us to think in new ways along uncharted territory. The Gurus did. What will Sikhs be like in the twenty-first century? Will the *Guru Granth* on floppy disks invoke the

same reverence? Will there be pizza or peanut butter sandwiches in our community kitchen and English ballads to the
accompaniment of guitars or banjos? Issues such as peace and
disarmament; divorce and family crises; birth control, abortion,
and the environment need to be discussed from the Sikh
perspective. Not that Sikhism takes hard or fixed positions on
these matters, but what kind of ethical framework does it give
to the Sikh so that he can make rational, intelligent and
responsible choices? Will we look to India for spiritual guidance
or will we feel self-sufficient here? Don't forget that we have a
new generation of Sikhs who were born and raised outside India
and may have only the weakest of links to the old country. While
traditions accommodate new needs and adapt to them, a sense
of continuity must remain.

Why do we venerate the past? Because the past is summed
up in the present, the future is implicit in it. What we are today
is because of what we have been, tomorrow we shall be no less
—because of what we are today. The past, present and the
future are interconnected, like three links of an unbreakable
chain. If those who do not remember the past are condemned
to repeat it, we have little choice but to recall and recollect the
past through tradition. But in our unquestioned respect for
tradition, I think we risk transforming Nanak the iconoclast into
an icon. (I see this in the increasing availability of the many wall
calendars with pictures of Guru Nanak or the gold pendants
with his likeness on them.) Tradition must remain a guide, a
friend, like the stars which show a seafaring man the way, like
a comfortable cocoon where we gather solace and which helps
define ourselves, never a jailer.

In the words of President Jimmy Carter, "We must adjust to
changing times and still hold true to unchanging principles."
Many of the circumstances that shaped our traditions may have
changed but to depart lightly from these habits of the heart
would be truly irreverent.

The Symbols of a Heritage

"History", as T.S. Eliot said "has many cunning passages, contrived corridors and issues...." Insofar as religions deal with people, places and events, they are amenable to historical analyses. But religions deal with a reality that transcends history — a reality that the senses cannot perceive and the intellect cannot fathom, yet with which the soul can commune. At that point in awareness, one is in the domain of faith. Faith is better than belief. In belief, someone else does the thinking for you; in faith, you accept the truth not at someone else's say-so, but because you have internalized it and endorsed it. Belief can mature into faith. From belief comes dependency; from faith, strength. The intangible realm of faith is a symbolic reality that is best expressed through symbols.

It is well to remember that the dimension of faith is not that of science. Of Man's many concerns, the deepest — faith — is symbolically expressed. By definition, symbols and signs signify something else beyond themselves, yet a symbol participates in defining the reality to which it points. A flag is not a nation but a symbol of it and attests to the shared history and dignity of a nation. That is why good people will fight and die for a flag but not let it be desecrated; it becomes significantly more in worth than the price of the cloth from which it is cut. A symbol, therefore, can't be easily replaced by another, or be subjected to scientific logic, nor can it be judged by the criteria of the marketplace.

Symbols are seen in every act of faith. They live and die but only after a historical catastrophe which greatly alters a people's

39

perception of self and their destiny. The death of existing symbols constitutes devastating events no less important than the phenomena that give them birth and shape. Symbols cannot be invented at will or intentionally produced by committees like business logos. They grow out of the collective consciousness of a people and have to be accepted by the subconscious dimension of their being. Their majesty and power lies in their symbolic character, not in any utilitarian value they might possess. Symbols are found in most aspects of man's creative activity — art, music, mathematics, history, religion. In fact, man's cultural history is often symbolically expressed. A cross is a symbol of Christ's suffering, not the reality of it. After 2,000 years of the Diaspora, the Jews seem to have recognized how symbols connect people to their roots; witness the growing popularity of the Lubavitchers.

India has produced many new religions — Buddhism, Jainism, Sikhism, among others. Of these, only Sikhism remains as a visible, active and distinct entity; others have reverted into the uneasy but comforting fold of Hinduism. Buddhism remains a powerful presence in Sri Lanka, Thailand, Myanmar, Vietnam, China and Japan, but not in the land of its birth—India.

John Kenneth Galbraith is correct in his somewhat facetious observation that anything that goes to India or develops there eventually gets Hinduized. He was talking of industry but it is equally true of religions. Islam in India is not quite the same as it is elsewhere, nor is Christianity. Sikhism too has lost some of its lustre and much of its pristine purity by its constant brushing with Hinduism. If Sikhism has not been absorbed into the Hindu fold entirely, it is not for want of trying by Hinduism, but due to two reasons: (a) its distinct philosophy which is at odds with and bluntly scornful of many Hindu practices, but that is a minor factor in its survival since most Sikhs are not well versed in it, and (b) the distinct external symbols of Sikhism which set the Sikhs apart in appearance and behavior.

Sometimes, I think that the rot in Sikhism had set in, but has been checked somewhat by the dramatic trauma to their psyche that occurred when the Indian Army attacked the Golden Temple and many other gurdwaras in 1984. In many ways, those events and the subsequent continuous state of war between India and the Sikhs has forced most Sikhs to reexamine their values and their sense of self. Many Sikhs who were no longer recognizable, became so by readopting the symbols of their faith. It was a horrendous price to pay for the Sikhs, but in the longer historical perspective, the benefits may be increased self-awareness.

The most visible aspects of Sikh tradition, and the most controversial are the external symbols. Not surprisingly, they generate the most intense internal debate and external concern. The interesting point is that only in Sikhism are such weighty and important matters debated by the laity. It is like "war being too important to be left to the Generals." The theologians and the clergy may preach and teach but the discussion is led and fueled by the ordinary folks who have to live the religion in the modern world; these people are on the frontlines and know the price, the problems, the frustrations as well as the rewards. And many of the people have never even taken the final vows (*Amrit*) of becoming Sikhs. It was just as true at the time of Guru Gobind Singh as it is now that many Sikhs never adopted all of the symbols of Sikhism but — like the Marrano Jews — kept their faith. Such *Sehajdhari* Sikhs have occupied an important and honorable place in Sikh history. But more about them another time.

There are many ways to look at Sikh symbols, the most popular way is to say: the Guru ordained them, ours is not to question why or what he meant by them. There is merit in that position. But the Guru did not bar us from thinking; so let us see what history can tell us. If symbols emerge out of shared history, how did we come to these five? And how has history affected them?

The Sikh with his external uniform and symbols is a Khalsa, a soldier in the army of God. This army created by Guru Gobind Singh was not made to rule over others or to shepherd a flock of sheep-like devotees. Unlike the army of Christ, where only the clergy were to be in uniform, in this army of the Khalsa, all followers were to join, all were to wear the uniform, everyone was always on call.

Though symbols are not to be judged by their utilitarian value, some of the Sikh symbols seem to be more functional than others. If long hair is *de rigueur*, a comb is essential for grooming, particularly for a people who knew no peace and lived on horseback. For a people fighting for survival, a sword as a weapon ensured survival. Again, befitting their life-style and India's terrain and weather, knee-length drawers were appropriate. A steel bracelet spoke of the strength of steel; its circle, of a life with no beginning and no end. This strong wide band of steel could also protect or be used as a weapon. In seventeenth century India, when there was a price on every Sikh's head, when a non-Muslim could not wear a turban, carry a weapon or ride a horse, when it was easier and more tempting to join the faceless anonymous hordes, the long-haired Khalsa boldly asserted their presence through their visible symbols. These symbols were a uniform of the Khalsa and still remain so. The philosophy of the Khalsa is eternal and the symbols represent it.

When I look at these symbols nearly three hundred years later, I see that most Sikhs have made a distinction even though at a subconscious level and look at symbols in two different tiers. Circumstances and times have indeed changed. The sword, the comb and the knee-length drawers were primarily utilitarian and seem to have changed the most with time. The sword that most Sikhs carry nowadays has been reduced to a symbolic level. Sometimes it is a dull blade a few inches long, more often it is a symbolic sword no more than an inch or two long attached to a comb or a pendant; at times it is only an impression of the sword inlaid into the wood of the comb. The sword has changed from a practical instrument of defence to a symbolic presence of that principle, of strength and resoluteness in action. Similarly, the knee-length drawers which were the only garment worn below a loose, long shirt have been modified by most Sikhs who wear the conventional underwear to go with other street attire. The comb though utilitarian has not changed all that much because it is still necessary for the long hair, although many Sikh women now carry only a small non functional miniature.

The steel bracelet and the long hair remain what they have always been — strictly symbolic. Professor Puran Singh likened the steel bracelet to a wedding band signifying the marriage of the Sikh to the Guru. However, a marriage is a sacrament only where there is real love; for many philanderers the bracelet, like the wedding band, can come on or off with equal ease. Others would rather lose a finger, a hand or a head than a wedding band. A Sikh surgeon would need to remove it and pocket it lest it tear the gloves. If the identity of a Sikh depended only on a visible bracelet, it would be easy for one to hide and that is not what Guru Gobind Singh intended. The long unshorn hair, strictly symbolic, with no pragmatic use or value in the marketplace remain the centerpiece of Sikh identity. It was true 300 years ago and remains equally true now.

One wonders what circumstances in history mandated that only the men adopt the turban to cover the long hair and not the women. The women do maintain all the Sikh symbols including the long unshorn hair. But in the Indian cultural milieu, without a turban they are not easily distinguishable from the millions of Indian women who are not Sikh. Certainly there is no bar to women wearing a turban and some Sikh women in India do; almost all of the Western converts to Sikhism do. For women, wearing of the turban over their long hair appears to have less to do with their understanding of Sikhism and more to do with the cultural constraints or with the particular school of thought or teacher who has influenced them. One need also remember that around the time that the Sikh symbols evolved, the Muslim rulers had barred non-Muslim men from wearing a turban. In the Indian culture, the turban for a man signified respect, irrespective of religion, women did not wear it. It was worn by a man who mattered and at that time, the emphasis of the rulers was to debase the subjects and deny them basic human dignity, self-worth and self-respect. The Gurus reversed this process and the turban, though not one of the five basic symbols of Sikhism, became inseparable from them, at least for the men.

To serve well, symbols must remain visible. Sometimes they are hidden much as the Marrano Jews found it necessary to hide their Jewishness when survival demanded it. Sikh symbols too can be easily concealed — all except the long, unshorn hair. That is precisely why in the annals of Sikh history, the unshorn hair have commanded the highest value. I don't know if Guru Gobind Singh so intended but in the subconscious dimension of their being, the Sikhs have somehow created a hierarchy of their symbols; the long unshorn hair have come to occupy the place of first among equals. A Sikh historically and now, declares his presence by this gift of his Guru. This is wholly consistent with the philosophic significance of a Sikh, and I venture to say that no matter how Sikhs change and what demands are placed upon them, as long as there are those who call themselves Sikhs, there will be long-haired Sikhs in the form that Guru Gobind Singh gave them. The dictum on the interdependence of form and function is significant and worthy of our attention.

A person gets from a symbol what he puts in it. It can be one man's comfort and inspiration as easily as another's jest and scorn. In the final analysis, symbols are an embodiment of history, not sentiment.

What is a Head Worth?

History tells us that in the sixteenth century Ignatius Loyola decreed that henceforth all priests of the Jesuit order must wear a collar. He also promulgated a special code of conduct for the clergy. Why? Apparently, Ignatius wanted to organize a special cadre of people devoted solely to serve the church and its flock. He called it the "army of Christ". This army of shepherds was to guide and lead the flock of believers. The uniform and the code defined the army. Those who joined this army pursued a higher calling than the laity.

What was India like around that time? A predominantly Hindu country, it was ruled by Muslims. Hindu society had always been caste-ridden in which over half the people were denied their humanity. For instance, women and lower castes could not read the holy scriptures and were denied access to most professions and trades etc. In that society, food was deemed defiled if the shadow of a lower caste person fell on it, and molten lead could be poured into the ears of such a person should he hear the sacred scriptures. Female infanticide was common and widows were routinely burnt at the pyres of the dead husbands in a rite called *suttee*. The upper castes were corrupt, the priests sold religious indulgences; the Brahmins were little better than charlatans, the ticket sellers for a dubious passage to heaven, but above all, the guardians of their own privileged lifestyles. The people were powerless, under the heel either of their own corrupt upper caste Brahmins or the ruling Muslims. The Muslims were intolerant of other religions, and by special taxation and other humiliations, waged a

45

full scale effort to islamize India. For instance, a non-Muslim could not bear arms or ride a horse except by special permission and paid special taxes for weddings and funerals.

History also tells us that on *Baisakhi* (around mid-April) 1699 the tenth Guru, Gobind, appeared before a congregation of 80,000 at Anandpur in Punjab. He flashed a naked sword and demanded a head. Some followers slipped away, many looked away. What kind of a Guru asks his followers for such a sacrifice? This Guru did, not once but five times. Each time, one sikh stepped forward.

History also records that from this modest beginning, Guru Gobind Singh created the mighty Khalsa nation. He dubbed them "lions", each equivalent to 125,000 ordinary men; each a king among men or a princess. His Sikhs were to have the valor of a lion and the grace of a princess. After he created this new order, the Guru knelt and his first five converts in turn converted him from Gobind Rai to Gobind Singh. By this act, he set himself, not as a ruler of a nation or the General of an army, but another soldier of the *Khalsa*. In this unique gesture, the leader acknowledged his debt to his own people - every leader is so indebted but few remember.

This incident deserves a special place in the annals of human history, management of large organizations, corporate hierarchy and leadership training. It was a rare process and technique to teach a downtrodden and powerless people the idiom of empowerment and it turned India's feudal society on its head. The lesson was not lost either on his Sikhs who cheerfully followed Guru Gobind Singh through the hell of pain, suffering and war, nor was it lost on the Hindu and Muslim elite of the society whose comfortable thrones were rocked by the Sikhs and who declared perpetual war on the Sikhs. I call this a perpetual war because even now three hundred years later in the twentieth century, India's feudal, Brahminical ruling classes resent the assertive sense of self and of power that the Guru bestowed upon his Sikhs. And therein lie the roots of the Sikh struggle for autonomy in India today.

History also tells us that where his followers had offered their heads, Guru Gobind Singh did not lag behind. He led his soldiers like a good General, not from a comfortable bunker but by being alongside them. He laid on the line not only all of his worldly possessions but also his family including minor children and ultimately his own life as well. He looked at the miracle of his creation of the Khalsa and attributed it to the *Khalsa*, without pride or conceit. God's work was done, he said. He gave his *Khalsa* a special code of conduct, a specific uniform, and distinctive symbols.

Khalsa was destined to be an army of winners, fearless and pure, in service to God and Man, in pursuit of righteousness. Unlike Ignatius Loyola's army, this "pride of lions" of Sikhs was to have no professional clergy, nor were there to be any sheep or shepherds. In this nation of soldiers of God, there were to be none who were more equal than others. Henceforth, every Sikh who was a Singh or Kaur was to be in uniform as a soldier. There was to be no higher calling for some and not for others, as Loyola had envisioned. The code of conduct applied equally to all, including the Guru and he himself remained answerable to the directives of his *Khalsa*.

Guru Gobind Singh created the *Khalsa* but the foundation stone had been laid by the iconoclast Nanak who challenged authority most boldly and by his followers who were martyred for the right to live with dignity. Guru Nanak found a demoralized nation of jackasses but by his teaching and by the examples of his followers, the spark of self-respect was lit; the process of transformation of a jackass into a lion had begun. Two hundred years later, by the time of Guru Gobind Singh, it was time to awaken the sleeping lion; the jackass had been metamorphosed. Only then did Guru Gobind Singh give the lion a new uniform and a code of conduct.

Guru Gobind Singh created an egalitarian order but for the ordinary follower he did not make the job any easier. If there is no clergy with binding ecclesiastical authority, then each Sikh has to cultivate and heed his own conscience. Each Sikh must hone his own intellect and plumb the depths of his own faith. Guru Gobind Singh recognized that each one of us has a constant battle to fight and the enemies are not necessarily out there. In all the battles of life that must be fought, no battlefield is more important than that of the mind. On that Baisakhi day three hundred years ago, Guru Gobind Singh staged the lesson of life: In everything you do and in each moment of your life, live honestly and so that you can put your head on the line. In whatever you do, do it so that you can live and die with dignity.

Now three hundred years after Guru Gobind Singh, is there anyone asking for a head?

When a business associate suggests that a little greasing of the palm could smooth the way for your project or when a prospective employer hints that a job or a promotion could be yours if you appear without your Sikh uniform, why should you resist? If the road you take is less than straight and narrow, why does it matter? If social life could be easier without the long hair or the Sikh uniform, why not take the easy road? Why look to the road less traveled by? Haven't times changed? Guru Gobind Singh is not asking for heads now, or is he?

Yes, three hundred years have passed. Guru Gobind Singh no longer appears in person at the job interview, flashing a naked sword and asking for your head. Mysterious are the ways of the Guru, and many are the people that he uses as his instruments. Now the question is framed differently, the flashing sword is replaced by the prospect of social isolation, economic disaster or harassment at the job or in the neighborhood. The instrument of the Guru is the affable man or woman behind the desk asking all these awkward questions. The instrument of the Guru may be the nice person having a cup of coffee or pleasant conversation with you. The intent of the questions is the same, only the form is different. The question is asked a hundred times a day and in a myriad ways. Three hundred years later, once again the Guru wants your head. Many will slip away, just as they did three hundred years ago. Many more will look away, just as they did then.

The question is: How are you going to answer the call?

Life and Death
—Some Random Thoughts

All living things must die. That is nature's law and there is no escaping it. Death, like taxes, is inevitable and one must come to terms with it. Even the Greeks and the ancient Hindus who prated about immortality and dreamed of it, finally succumbed. What then is eternal life? What is immortality? What is death to a Sikh? And how must a Sikh elect to die?

How one dies depends on how one lives, for all life leads to death. The whole teaching of Sikhism can be summed up in one question: How to live and die with dignity? Sikhism says that the best life is one that is devoted to the work ethic, sharing one's life with others, with an awareness of the infinite within so that the inner self is at peace with the world without. The rules for death must follow the rules for a good life. Unquestionably, the prayers, the mourning, the meetings, the wailing and crying, the wakes or whatever that we do, are not for the dead but for the living who need a rite of passage to transfer a life of purpose and activity to the realm of memories, to convert a painful present to a livable and memorable past.

This is the way of all flesh. It transcends culture, religion, history, and the bounds of geography. Are there any other ways of death? The only immortality is to have left the world a better and kinder place than the one we inherited. At birth, we inherit a flawed but tempting world. Usually, we are happy to inherit and enjoy its imperfect rewards, made possible by the work of generations past. Isn't our heritage then a debt from generations past to be paid to the future? At the same time, we recognize what we wish was different. So we gripe about the shortcomings of life and why shouldn't we? The only way to pay the debt of the good and the bad that is our inheritance is to leave the world a little better. This is no different from the man who enjoys the ripe mangoes from his father's fruit tree and now in turn plants one so that its fruit will nourish his children twenty years hence.

We are born, live an indeterminate span of life during which we pay our taxes and a mortgage or two and finally die, to be quickly forgotten; our fate—oblivion. No man is really dead until he is forgotten. A few achieve the immortality of being remembered beyond their span on earth. These are the true heroes, the ones that history remembers. They do not have to fight battles that boil the blood with weapons that guarantee pain and suffering. The most fierce battlefield is the self and the most potent weapon, one's mind.

What lies beyond death? Is there another world out yonder? Will one be resurrected whole from the worm-eaten remains or ashes? Will one burn in everlasting hell or enjoy dancing houris in heaven? Will our enemies return as cockroaches, earthworms or ugly bears to pester us, who have pestered them in life?

Most religions provide dogmatic certitude where only tentative hypotheses should suffice. The Socratic answer is not so bad that 'If there is a life after death, I will have the company of so many great men who have gone before me. If there is no life after death, it will be like a dreamless sleep; I am an old man and I need the rest.' A Buddhist may chose to think in terms of nothingness. The traditional Hindu propitiates the past and prays for a better future. Is he even aware of the present? The existentialist has little use for the past and less hope for the future, he only knows the present. The Judeo-Christian concept of original sin is not found in Sikh belief, nor is the idea of someone else atoning for our sins or dying for them, such as the claim for Christ's suffering on the cross. The sin would lie not in eating from the tree of knowledge but in not using that

knowledge for leaving the world a little better. Eventually
when my bills come due, payment is going to be extracted from
me, not someone else. In the Sikh view, the human life is
looked at as a boon, a unique opportunity, a gift from God, to be
lived productively in honest labor with sincere service to
humanity, and with a mind centered on the Infinite within us.
At the end of life, one needs to answer the perennial questions,
"O mortal, what did you do to transcend the self in this unique
life?" Was the finite, mortal shell of flesh put to good use? This
crumbling, decaying flesh houses the immortal spirit, the
divine spark and is the vehicle for it. Did it fulfill its responsibility?

But time is like three links of a chain connecting the past,
present and the future, except that the only link we can see and
steer is that of the present, and that also imperfectly. The past
is dead and buried, the future yet unborn. We are what we are
because of what was, we will be because of what we are now.
Therefore, if one lives fully in the present, the future will
automatically be well. Death be not proud, one could say. One
could also take a hint from Norman Vincent Peale, the prophet
of positivism. Since no man, he argues, knows his life before
birth, the developmental intra-uterine period, is the infant
happy to be born, to leave a comfortable universe of the womb
for the unknown world outside? Is the fetus even aware of the
world outside? The developing human has no opinion on it for
he knows nothing of it. Similarly, no man may speak of what lies
beyond this life as we know it, yet like a newborn, one must
accept it. For the newborn, life outside the mother's womb is
an unknown reality, for us the reality after death is equally
obscure. It will be different but it will be good. Life and death
— two stages of existence with a veil separating them through
which we may not see.

Let us now switch gears to focus on a different dimension of
life and death. All kinds of fish live in the sea, some are so small

that the naked eye can barely see them. Others ply the ocean in total darkness at a depth where no light penetrates and no eye can make out their shapes; they must supply their own light to attract food. It is not possible to shoot them or spear them. But there is an easier way to decimate them. All one has to do is to remove them from the environment that gives them life. A fine and capacious net can do that indiscriminately to a large number, quickly and economically. All one has to do is to remove the organism from its source of sustenance.

There are all kinds of people in this world, some good, some bad. But there are very few Sikhs. A Sikh is like that fish in the ocean except his sea is that of *gurbani* and his heritage. *Gurbani* — the *Guru Granth* — is what gives him life, sustains him, nurtures him and makes him a Sikh. Without it, he is spiritually dead — like the fish out of water.

The essence of the Sikh way of life lies in honest and honorable conduct in all matters with a mind in equipoise. One can see God in the self only when one can see him in another. The crux of the matter is to realize that the hungry person is you, the destitute is you, not some him or her apart from you with a separate reality. In separateness, we die. So that the good you do is not because you should, but because of what you are. Then you become an instrument of God, a part of Guru-consciousness — an irresistible force.

In living a life as an instrument of God, the fear of death is lost. This is what Sikhism teaches. Look at the number of martyrs that such a tiny minority as the Sikhs have produced. During the many years that India struggled for Independence from the British, over two-thirds of all Indians sentenced to life-imprisonment or death by the British were Sikhs. And Sikhs form barely two percent of India's teeming millions.

Isn't it amazing that for almost all of the 500 years of their existence, Sikhs have been locked in one battle or another for survival? There were times when their number was so small that the governments of the day, like smug cats licking their paws, proudly declared that all Sikhs had been exterminated. But the Sikh spirit was immortal; some Sikhs always surfaced to boldly belie the claim. All armies fighting the Sikhs — from the Mughals and the British to the armed hordes of present-day Indian governments — realized that guns and bombs can kill many Sikhs but Sikhism does not die. There are always more to continue the struggle. How best to destroy them?

There are easier ways. All one has to do is to remove the Sikh from *gurbani*, his source of sustenance and he or she is quickly and automatically reduced to an empty shell — a person without a focus, running amok like a frightened and cornered rat who will soon self-destruct.

Luckily for our enemies, Sikhism is relatively young. Our history is turbulent, our ties to the dominant culture of Hinduism old and strong. Many Sikhs are unsure of their identity and ignorant of Sikh heritage and teachings. Many Sikhs are poorly educated. To manipulate them is easy. All one needs to do is to cast doubts on their early history. That part of the record is so unclear anyway. Where is the proof that Guru Nanak ever founded a new order or travelled anywhere? Where is clear incontrovertible evidence that Guru Gobind Singh ever established the Khalsa the way we believe he did or wanted to? Transform this history into legend and myth, draw parallels with Hindu mythology and soon the origins of Sikhism would be as hazy as are the beginnings of Hinduism. Better yet, reduce it to an unrecognizable limb of Hinduism so that its identity is lost and its vitality sapped. It has happened before; Buddhism is no longer a major religion in India, the land of its birth.

The Sikhs in Punjab are justifiably angry with India because its successive governments have treated them shabbily and cruelly. Why not turn these angry Sikhs to un-Sikh activities? Arm them, encourage them to loot and kill. Let them think that by killing innocents they are avenging the wrongs done to them.

Use all the sophisticated Madison Avenue techniques to brand them as terrorists to the world. They will soon self-destruct.

Does that sound familiar? You bet it does! Is it happening now? Indeed! There is only one possible way out of this impasse. Like the fish, we have to avoid the net that is cast for us and swim within the life-giving sea of *gurbani*.

Before we give a press statement, before we write a letter or raise a slogan, before we kidnap someone, plant a bomb or squeeze a trigger, even before we build another gurdwara, let each Sikh ask one question and only one question: Would the Guru approve of what I am about to do? That is the categorical imperative. Or else we become like the fish out of water.

Parshad-The
Mystical Communion?

Some years ago, I escorted a young non-Sikh woman to a Sikh religious service. Although born a Christian, she was fond of eastern religions, and had some knowledge of India and Hinduism. The basic Sikh service is pretty much the same the world over and for any occasion — some singing of liturgy, an optional lecture or exposition of history or scripture, congregational prayer, and to conclude, *parshad* and a simple community meal which are offered to everybody. The *parshad* is obligatory to every service, the community meal is sometimes lacking if the facilities do not permit it.

The *parshad* as well as the community meal are usually prepared and distributed by volunteers from the congregation. That day two volunteers were distributing *parshad*. My friend refused to accept it from one and preferred that it be given by the other. She insisted that one of the volunteers had a more spiritual aura and *parshad* from his hands would be more meaningful. Some Sikhs nearby tried to assuage her feelings by suggesting that it was only a '*halvah*-like dessert' and she could enjoy it as such, no matter who distributed it. We escaped the confusion but the incident stayed with me. What after all is *parshad*? Is it only a dessert? Is it like communion in a Church? If a non-Sikh accepts it, is his belief compromised? Would it matter who handed it?

I remember being invited to a church some years earlier where the minister made a point of requesting that only the believers in Christianity should partake of the communion. I recall many of the stringent requirements that apply to a Roman Catholic as he steps forward to receive communion. I realize that some of these have been relaxed somewhat in the past fifteen years. At communion, a wafer of bread and a thimbleful of wine or juice is offered to the believer in memory of Christ's sacrifice on the cross. There are clearly defined criteria to determine if the individual is in good standing and qualifies to receive communion. At one time, the Roman Catholic Church used to require a believer to refrain from food or sex for at least 12 hours and confess his or her transgressions before stepping up to the altar to receive communion. Also, keep in mind that only a priest may consecrate the bread and wine, not even a nun has that privilege, much less a lay person. A nun may distribute it but a lay person may not. It is a matter of dogma to a Christian that the bread and wine are 'transubstantiated' into the flesh and blood of Christ in memory of Christ and not merely symbolic of them. This stems from the "doctrine of the real presence of Christ in the Eucharist," dating between 1546 to 1563 from the Council of Trent, which debated and codified many issues of Christian belief. Following this dogma, the appearance of bread and wine remains but the "reality" of the substance changes and becomes flesh and blood of Christ.

How do Sikhs view the *parshad*? What is *parshad* and what is it not? More often than not, it is made of wheat flour, butter, sugar and water cooked to a pudding-like consistency. This is the traditional composition but *parshad* can be anything suitable for the congregation to share and eat. At times, it has been jaggery, sugar, grain, fruit, nuts or cookies, salt, among other things — whatever a person could afford and whatever was available in the house. It does not have to be much for it is not meant to assuage physical hunger; less than a spoonful would do. The traditional preparation has 500 years of history behind it, and at all gurdwaras and most places where it is possible, this version prevails. The *parshad* need not be cooked at the gurdwara. In smaller congregations where cooking facilities are lacking, it is often cooked at somebody's home and brought in for distribution. Predictably, the traditional composition draws upon ingredients which would normally be found in any Punjabi home, even the poorest one. That it tastes like a good dessert is all the better, for who can resist it?

History and tradition have given the Sikhs a novel timer to determine when the flour is sufficiently cooked: the time it takes to chant the *Japuji* (the morning prayer) at a methodical but leisurely pace. The aroma of *parshad* being prepared pervades the area and is sufficient to bind the Sikhs to their heritage and culture. One must never underestimate the pull and power of nostalgia.

In the Sikh view, anybody may cook, serve or receive *parshad*. For either of the three: preparer, server or receiver, no questions are asked and no criteria or qualifications are imposed. One need not even be a nominal Sikh, much less one in good standing. One may not be asked when the last sin was committed, prayers uttered, nor his or her status, caste, or belief. What is required is that the *parshad* be served in a dignified manner and respectfully accepted.

It is important to point out that anybody can make or serve *parshad* — a woman, a non-Sikh, a sinner or a saint — none may be barred. This is significant when you realize that in many religions, a woman may not read the scriptures or lead the prayers, particularly if she is menstruating. Since Sikhism does not advocate a life of renunciation, sexual activity in a marriage is never any bar to full religious participation. Salvation must be sought in this worldly life — a domestic life, honestly led, shared with the community and spent with an awareness of the Infinite within.

The *parshad* from one place or gurdwara is not more sacred than from another. Often Sikhs give special reverence to *parshad* from a historical gurdwara such as the Golden Temple in Amritsar and are more cavalier about it from a small, new, unknown place or from somebody's home. Such distinctions are utter nonsense. What sanctifies *parshad* and lifts it from the level of a *halvah*-like dessert to a sacramental communion is not where it was made nor the person who makes or serves it but the congregation in mindful prayer and ultimately, the attitude of the receiver. The *parshad* is not lessened in value if a sinner makes, takes or serves it; he or she is ennobled by the aura of a congregation in mindful prayer.

There are only two ways to devalue *parshad*: with unhygienic unwashed hands of the preparer, server or receiver or by the wandering mind of the receiver. The personality and character of the individuals neither diminish nor exalt the significance of *parshad*; however, the experience of the blessing may inspire and elevate the individual. For a Sikh, the significance of *parshad* is deeply ingrained in his marrow through 500 years of history. A Sikh deems it a blessing to make it, a blessing to serve it, a blessing to receive it with all humility. Nobody turns it down for who wants to turn down a grace? Life is tough enough already.

Many are the ways to reach and know God, the Infinite within us all. But all roads meander through the reality of the inner self. The congregation attuned to that common reality creates a *parshad* which is a product of the Sikh psyche but not limited exclusively to the Sikh spiritual needs. Others who accept it need not fear for their identity. A Christian may accept it in the name of Jesus and many Hindus and Muslims particularly in the Punjab have been addicted to it for generations but have remained Hindus or Muslims. He who feels part of the blessing will benefit; he who doesn't, won't.

In the right spiritual atmosphere what is transformed or transubstantiated is not *parshad* but the minds of those who receive it. For them, it becomes a holy communion. If communion is sacramental sharing, then *parshad* becomes that, but it is never the communion defined in the Christian doctrine and experience. For many, *parshad* remains a *halvah*-like dessert and never becomes anything more. For them, it may be fattening but usually there is not enough of it and so are many of the other good things in life. To think that *parshad* is merely another dessert is like thinking that glass and diamond are the same for they both shine.

What is in a Name?

What for heaven's sake is so complicated about naming a baby?
You made it; you can give it any moniker you wish. The little
brat can even change it later! Easier yet, the local bookstore
undoubtedly stocks books which list thousands of names for
boys and girls and even rank them áccording to their popularity.
One can select the trendiest, most fashionable name just as one
chooses designer jeans by the label and by social acceptability.

Let us look at this somewhat differently. Amongst all of
God's creations, human birth is indeed special. The opportunity granted to the human is unique. A way is presented to
discover God by serving man — by leaving the world a better
place. We enjoy all that the world has to offer. We inherit an
imperfect world bequeathed to us as God's creation. The
generations past have made this world what it is today. What
mark we leave behind us will be the legacy of the generations
to come. The debt we inherit from our forefathers we pay to óur
children who, in turn, will repay theirs.

With that point in view, a child becomes the most exquisite
and mystical of God's gifts. Nowhere else is there such a perfect
blending of the mystery of God and the free will of man. The
past is inherent in the child and this new child carries us into
eternity, thus representing all of the future that is yet to be. The
past, present and the future, all merge flawlessly and effortlessly in the child. With that attitude governing us, the act of
naming a child in the Sikh tradition becomes simple yet
meaningful and purposeful, but most importantly, an easily
understood rite.

Recognizing that a child is no less than the greatest of God's gifts to man, the first step in arriving at a name is a prayer of thanksgiving. Next, the Sikh opens the *Guru Granth* at random and identifies the first letter of the first hymn on the left—hand page. Why the left—hand page? Because we write from left to right. We are merely letting God guide us in finding the letter for the name by not selectively culling a favorite hymn. The idea is to let go of our ego and will, and recognize the necessity and beauty in surrender to the will of God. In essence, this act says: "Thy will be done and let my child's name (and life) be guided by the holy spirit as this child begins a new life."

In the Sikh way of life, this sense of surrender to the will of God is inseparably intertwined with the prayerful and vigorous efforts of man. In the next step, therefore, we the human parents, relatives and friends make up a suitable name based on the letter gifted to us from the *Guru Granth*. Whereas the selection of the letter unites the child to the will of God from whom all things flow, our construction of a name from that letter merges the child with our hopes, dreams and aspirations. Usually, therefore, the name is selected to be phonetically pleasing, or to represent qualities that we aspire for the child — attributes of heroic dimensions, saintly virtues, memorable beauty, qualities of the heart and mind or familial continuity and lineage, etc. In my daughter's case—for instance, the first names of her two grandmothers are combined in her first name, which is thus a combination of two distinct cultural traditions, Indian and American.

There is another very important part to every Sikh's name — 'Kaur' or princess for every girl and 'Singh' or lion for a boy. This part of the name links the child to its heritage. This part — 'Singh or Kaur' — needs some elaboration, for its use is not without some controversy nor is it consistent among present day Sikhs. Not so long ago, I was talking to a bright, idealistic, articulate young Sikh woman who was visibly upset by this apparent gender difference in naming a child. Why did the Guru make men into lions but only princesses out of women? Were the women not good enough or strong enough? I had thought about it before, but not very much and not too deeply. I had to admit that she had a point. But during the discussion, we both saw that as a man I too could take umbrage. Did the Guru think that a man was only a beast even though a king of the jungle while a woman was like royalty, graceful and born to rule?

Perhaps both views are immature. History tells us that there have been many heroic women and cowardly men among Sikhs, as among others. And the Gurus were creating an egalitarian society, liberating women from their bondage of centuries. If men and women are like two sides of a coin which complement each other to make a true coin, then to identify some of their generic attributes *per se* does not demean either sex or any individual, but merely points out that the two sexes are distinct though equal. Certainly there is nothing derogatory in being either a princess or a lion for each is the top of the heap in its own category.

"Many speak of courage, speaking cannot give it" — so goes a song popular with many young Sikhs. Further along, the song continues: "One does not become royal by birth but only if one's home is Anandpur Sahib." Here one is speaking of Anandpur as the spiritual home of a Sikh for that is where Guru Gobind Singh created the Khalsa over 300 years ago. In other words, if a Sikh was to have the courage of a lion and the grace of royal stock, it would be by following the Sikh spiritual way and not by bounds or distinctions of family, gender or birth. Becoming a Sikh free in spirit, resolute in action — and that is the essence of 'Singh' or 'Kaur'.

Historically, only Singh or Kaur are used to distinguish a male name from that of a female. No gender difference exists and no sexual distinction or identification is traditionally made in the first or given name. The traditional first name among Sikhs is absolutely gender-neutral. One cannot ignore, however, the increasing use of gender-specific first names among Sikhs which is a relatively recent phenomenon; this trend undoubtedly is indicative of the predominantly non-Sikh cultural milieu in which we live. The roles that men and women play as responsible, ethical individuals in life are not defined by Sikh names but are determined by their own individual circumstances.

By rejecting the further appellation and identification of caste to the name, the Sikh emphasizes the equality of all people. One becomes high or low not by birth, caste, family, status or wealth but by righteous living in which the spiritual self and the life of action are inseparably merged much as water and milk become one on mixing.

Ultimately, to name a child in the Sikh tradition is to say: Here is a child of God, given unto a family's love and care, a maker of destinies of peoples and nations.

The Sikh Marriage
(*Anand Karaj*)

The Sikh attitude to all ceremonies and rituals is simple: only that act is sacred which is performed with an awareness of the Infinite and of the mystical presence of God within the individual and the congregation. The two essential items of a social or public act, therefore, become: (a) the *Guru Granth*, the holy book of the Sikhs which is indeed a book but is more than that, it is the Guru and thus the essence of all spiritual authority; and (b) the presence of a community of followers — the congregation — in which resides all temporal authority. These essentials apply to all Sikh ceremonies ranging from birth to death.

The marriage ceremony in all cultures historically has two elements: first, a spiritual component to indicate that these two individuals have embarked on a lifelong path which defines the family — the fundamental unit of all civilized societies, and in which the two individuals will create a whole which is greater than the sum of the parts. The primary family unit is like a bird that does not fly on one wing alone. Secondly, the marriage ceremony is a binding contractual declaration to society which has legal, economic and societal implications.

The Sikh marriage ceremony is consistent with these principles. In the Punjabi language, it is called *Anand Karaj*, meaning the ceremony of bliss. It is truly a sacrament of joy. Symbolically, the witnesses to the ceremony are God and the community

There are a few simple elements to the *Anand Karaj*. All

Sikh ceremonies require a congregation, mindful prayer and the *Guru Granth*. The marriage ceremony, like all other Sikh ceremonies, can be performed by any adult, male or female. The ceremonial functions are not restricted to the ordained ministry. Recognizing that this couple is setting forth on a new venture of fundamental importance, the Sikhs have traditionally performed this ceremony in the early hours of the morning. Much as dawn speaks of a day to come, the marriage ceremony points to a lifetime to be. However, this is tradition, not canon. Any day, and any hour of the day, is auspicious. The attitude of supplication and an awareness of the sacred make any time a good omen. No astrological forecasting for the right day and time of marriage is necessary.

Sensitivity to the importance of the event, which indicates for a couple the threshold of a new phase in life requires that the ceremony be held in circumstances which enhance its aura: early in the morning, in clean surroundings whether it be a Sikh temple (gurdwara), home or a rented hall, in a place free of drugs, alcohol, tobacco or other intoxicants. Again, we look to tradition, common sense and human feelings to support such practice and not to religious doctrine.

Barriers of race, caste or class are not recognized. Again, in this I recognize that Sikhs have not remained untouched by the majority influence around them. Unfortunately, therefore, though most Sikhs acknowledge that it is wrong, many look at the caste affiliation, at least superficially; most Jats appear to observe such distinctions even more stringently. I have never been able to understand or reconcile myself to the vestiges of this pernicious practice amongst the Sikhs. Marriage occurs only when the individuals have reached the age of consent, freely consent to marry and are willing and able to shoulder its responsibilities. In this matter, as in all others, men and women enjoy equal rights and equal obligations. Exchange of gifts between the groom and bride and their respective families is permitted; however, dowry is not since it undermines human dignity.

In the Indian cultural milieu as well as in the Sikh view, a marriage is just not two people who decide they like each other, will have two-three children, pay the requisite mortgage and their share of taxes while they disappear into the sunset to live happily ever after, as in a B movie from Hollywood. Since the family is the fundamental unit of civilized society, a marriage represents a merger of two families. In marriage, one family does not lose a child (son or daughter) but acquires another. A merger can be successful only if there is some common basis for it. The first step in marriage, therefore, is for the two families to meet and arrive at a mutual appreciation of each other — educational background, social status, economic realities and religious persuasion, etc. In life, these factors often shape individual habits and attitudes which determine compatibility. The most sophisticated computer would have grave difficulty catching and matching the subtle nuances of differences which can make the difference between success and failure, heaven and hell.

During the marriage ceremony, the blessings of God and the best wishes of the community (congregation) are invoked. Compared to most Christian weddings, the bride's father symbolically hands or gives away his daughter by placing each end of a sash in the hands of the bride and groom. Actually, the Sikh concept is different — the sash signifies the joining together of the two individuals; it is a knot connecting the two. The ceremony itself involves four circumambulations of the holy book. At each perambulation, one of the four prescribed hymns in turn is read and then sung. The essence of the hymns and of the ceremony is to emphasize that the life of wedded bliss (that of a householder) is complete when, in all its activities, it is resplendent with an awareness of God. For a Sikh, salvation lies not in a life of renunciation but in a life of honest labor and service as a householder. In the first circling, the marriage rite has begun. In the second circling, divine music is heard. In the third circling, the love of God has been awakened and in the fourth, the marriage ceremony has been completed in an awareness of the eternal God.

The Sikh marriage ceremony was initiated by Guru Ram Das, the fourth Guru. The ceremony symbolizes that there are four steps to the development of a harmonious marriage: mutual respect, love, restraint and harmony. The four hymns and the four perambulations of the *Guru Granth* by the couple reflect their acknowledgement of these four steps. The hymns do not speak of marital duties, household chores or other mundane matters which intelligent, educated couples would work out between themselves according to their particular circumstances. Instead, the hymns look at the development of the spiritual relationship between man and God as the metaphor for the ideal relationship. This becomes clear from the writings of Guru Angad when he said: "A union of bodies is no union, however close it may be; it is only when souls meet, can we speak of a union true." His follower, Guru Amar Das had also expressed similar views in his writings.

Historians disagree on when the Sikh ceremony came to be widely used and when it became legally recognized. Although the hymns that are traditionally used at the *Anand Karaj* were composed by Guru Ram Das, some say that the Sikh ceremony had evolved earlier in the time of Guru Amar Das, his predecessor. It acquired legal status in India in 1909 by virtue of the Anand Marriage Act. One must remember though that until very recently many ceremonies, formalities and rites within the Indian cultural context were recognized by the community and had legally binding status without the formal paperwork which is the hallmark of a legal document as we know it now. For instance, most of us who were born in India 30 or more years ago have no birth certificates, and it is doubtful that our parents who were married 40 or 50 years ago can produce a   marriage certificate. Yet, the individual commitment and the community's recognition provided the framework for the family structure within the Indian cultural setting. But these matters are best left to historians and sociologists.

The Sikh view of marriage is emphatically not in step with the biblical injunction: "As the Church is subject to Christ let the wives we subject to their husbands in all things." In many places in their writings and by many examples, the Gurus emphasized a relationship based on equality, love, respect and sharing. The unequal and inferior status of women prevalent in Indian society was clearly rejected by the teachings of Sikhism. The Sikh code of conduct decrees the same ceremony for the remarriage of widows and widowers. This is important when one realizes that in the traditional Hindu practice, widows were either cremated alive with their dead husbands or not allowed to remarry.

The Sikh marriage echoes the Christian view of matrimony and family, popularly cited as: "What God hath united, let no man put asunder." Though marriage may be made in heaven, it must be lived here on earth, and sometimes divorce becomes necessary. That is a serious societal matter and there is no religious ceremony to sanction it. It is handled according to social custom and secular law.

Food Taboos in Sikhism

The first response to the title of this essay is predictable: certainly there are no food taboos in Sikhism. This is after all a young, modern, vibrant faith, very practical in its doctrines and sensible in its beliefs. But there is always a hooker. What set me thinking about food restrictions was something that happened about twenty-five years ago; I have heard periodic echoes of the issue over the years. For about three months, I was the Secretary of our major and at that time the only gurdwara in New York. We used to meet once a month, then it became once a week. More regular in attendance than any others were some young, single Sikhs, mostly students, living in the city. I think what attracted them was the socializing and the free community lunch that always followed the service. I could relate to that and to them. Often we would spend half a Sunday at the gurdwara and then gather at someone's apartment to shoot the breeze and solve the problems of the world.

One day a group of young friends volunteered to provide the community lunch following the weekly service. Of course, they would not prepare a traditional meal but offered to serve ham and cheese sandwiches instead. I thought it was a great idea. When I broached it to the management committee, however, all hell broke loose. How could I think of sandwiches, I was asked? I offered pizza but the reaction was not much better. I was told in no uncertain terms that the meal must be a simple Punjabi meal — vegetables, beans, unleavened flat bread (*chappatties*). Rice could be added or substituted for the bread, if necessary. Accompaniment of pickle and a good dessert would round up

70

the menu. The preparations did not have to be simple and, depending upon the host, could be elaborate, but the menu was to be strictly vegetarian and under no circumstances was it to depart substantially from the traditional Punjabi meal.

I too adore Punjabi food and more so with each passing year that I live outside a Punjabi milieu. But I wonder at the unwritten code on food proscription that seems to operate at Sikh gatherings. Where in Sikh history or theology does it say that all meals are to be vegetarian or prepared in a particular way? And following religious services at homes, I have partaken of community meals which were so extensive and elaborate that they would rival the spread at the fanciest restaurant. Such a feast raises the obvious question: is that what the Guru intended when he initiated the concept of a community meal (*langar*) following a religious service?

History provides us some sensible ways of looking at what we believe and what we practice. Indeed Sikhs observe no food taboos as are found among the Jews, Muslims or Hindus, among others. Of the two dominant religions in India, the Hindus eat no beef while the Muslims will not come near pork. The Sikhs find common ground by finding both kinds of flesh acceptable. It is true, nevertheless, that a great majority of Sikhs do not eat beef since many of them come from a Hindu background. In fact in Punjab, before India was partitioned in 1947, neither beef nor pork was easily available in deference to the strong beliefs of the two majority religions. Also many, if not most Hindus are obligatory vegetarians. (Observing Jains eat no eggs or onions either.) Consequently, most Sikhs never acquired a taste for either beef or pork but are content with chicken, mutton or lamb. Landlocked Punjab does not have much of a variety in fish, but it is enjoyed in the limited quantity that it is available. Throughout Sikh history, there have been movements or subsects of Sikhism which have espoused vegetarianism. I think there is no basis for such dogma or practice in

Sikhism. Certainly Sikhs do not think that a vegetarian's achievements in spirituality are easier or higher. It is surprising to see that vegetarianism is such an important facet of Hindu practice in light of the fact that animal sacrifice was a significant and much valued Hindu Vedic ritual for ages.

Guru Nanak in his writings clearly rejected both sides of the arguments — on the virtues of vegetarianism or meat eating — as banal and so much nonsense, nor did he accept the idea that a cow was somehow more sacred than a horse or a chicken. He also refused to be drawn into a contention on the differences between flesh and greens, for instance. History tells us that to impart his message, Nanak cooked meat at an important Hindu festival in Kurukshetra. Having cooked it he certainly did not waste it, but probably served it to his followers and ate himself. History is quite clear that Guru Hargobind and Guru Gobind Singh were accomplished and avid hunters. The game was cooked and put to good use, to throw it away would have been an awful waste.

Sikhs also do not respond to the semitic commandment on avoiding animals with cloven hoofs. And one semitic practice clearly rejected in the Sikh code of conduct is eating flesh of an animal cooked in ritualistic manner; this would mean kosher and *halal* meat. The reason again does not lie in religious tenet but in the view that killing an animal with a prayer is not going to ennoble the flesh. No ritual, whoever conducts it, is going to do any good either to the animal or to the diner. Let man do what he must to assuage his hunger. If what he gets, he puts to good use and shares with the needy, then it is well used and well spent, otherwise not.

The community meal (*langar*) that the Sikhs serve in their gurdwaras has several purposes. Much of India even now is bound in traditions of caste. In the Hindu caste system, the high and the low castes do not mix socially, do not eat from the same kitchen. The food of a Brahmin is considered defiled if the shadow of an untouchable falls upon it. Sikhism set out to break these barriers. In the gurdwara, the meal is served to people who sit in a row. You may not chose who to sit next to; it may even be an untouchable. You may not ask to be served by someone special. The food is prepared by volunteers from the community in a community kitchen. Men, women and children, rich and poor alike, work together to cook and to serve. This is where young and old, children and adults learn the concept of service. The food is available to all; kings and the homeless have partaken of it. Akbar who ruled India in the sixteenth century enjoyed such a meal. In this country, most gurdwaras do not have *langar* service operating all day but one that serves only one meal at the conclusion of a service. Therefore, whatever food is left over is either carted home by those who wish, or is delivered to a center for the needy. In the sixties, many hippies trekking through India found gurdwaras an easy place for a quick and free meal; countless homeless people enjoy this Sikh hospitality every day. It is a way for the ordinary Sikh to thank God from whom all blessings flow. Service to the needy and sharing one's blessings with others is a cornerstone of the Sikh way of life and it starts in the community kitchen. It is a recognition of the principle that even God has little meaning or relevance to an empty belly. The prayers of the congregation and their spirit of service make the meal special, not the variety in the menu.

The usual menu in a gurdwara is simple — one vegetable, some beans, a handful of rice and one or two pieces of flat bread (*chappatties*). This is what the poorest people in Punjab eat. The ingredients are what the simplest home in Punjab would have. Fancier dishes are avoided even if one can afford them for the purpose is not to instill envy in others or to show off one's own riches. If meat is avoided, it is not because of any canon but because the menu should be such that everybody can afford and anybody can eat; something nobody will have any compunctions or reservations about. Remember that gurdwaras are open to all and often frequented by Hindus and Muslims alike. The menu for the *langar* at the gurdwara has to provide the least common denominator in the Indian cultural tradition.

I have heard there are a few, rare gurdwaras in India where meat is served at times. I emphasize that such gurdwaras are few and in them, service of meat is rare. I suppose the practice started sometime ago and has continued. No harm in it as long the people coming there are aware of it. It is not a matter of Sikh doctrine but of consideration for others and common sense. Some historians contend that meat was often served in *langar* at the time of Guru Angad. History has it that Guru Amar Das, well before he became a Guru, visited Guru Angad. On that day, some Sikh had donated a large quantity of fish which was being served in the community meal. Amar Das had been a devout Hindu and a vegetarian until that time. Some historians say that he was somewhat squeamish about it but, now that he had become a Sikh, accepted the fish as a gift from the Guru's kitchen. Others suggest that Guru Angad, knowing full well that Amar Das was a vegetarian, directed the *sevadars* not to offer him the fish. Considering the love of nature and of God's creation in the writings of the Gurus, wanton killing of animals would not be condoned, nor would be their ritual sacrifice for gustatory satisfaction or otherwise.

There are other benefits to a simple but sufficient lunch after a service. The attendees know that they do not have to rush home and feed the kids or themselves. The mind is not distracted by the chores waiting at home; time off from them is a welcome respite, however brief. One can relax and enjoy the service single-mindedly.

Hindus have often debated if what you eat determines your spiritual status. Sikhs do not believe that. With such practical and liberal reasoning, some strange and unorthodox practices can also arise. Khushwant Singh speaks of a gurdwara in

Australia which serves beer with the food. Given Sikh history and teaching, that just wouldn't do. In his many writings, Guru Nanak offered only two criteria for food taboos, both are based on common sense. Anything that will harm the body or mind is to be shunned. And all things edible are available and permissible in moderation.

Over the years, I have seen many variations on the theme but to discuss and debate unnecessarily what to eat or not to eat in Sikhism is to transform what a modicum of intelligence and common sense can easily resolve into a mesh with the complexity of the Gordion knot.

Who is a Sikh?

These days it has become fashionable to apply two litmus tests to the definition of a Sikh. One is that of political correctness. We have all been to Sikh gatherings where, if your views fall even a hair short of an independent Sikh homeland, you are quickly branded 'anti-Sikh.' The currently precarious position among Sikhs of the well-known writer Khushwant Singh is an example. It seems to me from my rudimentary understanding of Sikhism that the religion allows and even encourages a virtual rainbow of shades of opinions. This is true in theory, the practice often leaves one aghast.

If Zail Singh, the former Indian President is branded a quisling, I can understand. In his official capacity, he issued the orders approving the invasion of the Golden Temple and many other Gurdwaras in Punjab on Guru Arjan's martyrdom day in June 1984. His poor judgement and moral cowardice opened a new chapter on state terrorism against the Sikhs and brought India close to fragmentation. A sense of self-respect as a Sikh would have required that the papers he signed be of his resignation. But I am reminded that over the 500 years of our history, many Sikhs in responsible positions have acted abominably. After the Jallianwala Bagh massacre in 1919, Sikh religious leaders at the Akal Takht honored the responsible General O'Dyer. Almost 200 years ago, some Sikh rulers sided with Muslim hordes against Sikh armies. Two years ago, some Sikhs of Delhi honored H.K.L. Bhagat, the man who may have masterminded the massacre of the Sikhs in 1984. The Sikhs have a right to be furious with these people but the fact that they were Sikhs cannot be denied.

In my view, if Khushwant Singh or Patwant Singh, respectable writers both, fail to publicly endorse the idea of Khalistan, that does not make them any less as Sikhs. You can be furious with them. You can call them misguided or misinformed and they can return the compliment, but to disavow them as Sikhs is grossly unfair. There are many honest Sikhs in that category — General Aurora and Air Marshall Arjan Singh come to mind. Their anguish at how brutally and inhumanely the Indian Government has treated the Sikhs is not any less than yours or mine. How the personal lifestyles of these or any other people would stand scrutiny is a different matter indeed, but Sikhs should have other criteria for evaluating each other. And that would raise another question — who has the right and the competence to judge?

For many years, Sikhs political leaders like Longowal or Simranjit Singh Mann sought a solution within the framework of the Indian Constitution. It is only now that Mann seems to have despaired of the notion of a unified Indian nation. Yet, no one can deny that his sacrifice in the cause of the Sikhs is clear and significant. Bhindranwale undeniably showed Sikhs how to die with dignity and honor. But in his short life he never raised the slogan for an independent Khalistan, though he has now become the inspiration for its struggle. This is because circumstances have changed. Whereas only a few years ago, it was possible for Sikhs to conceive of a productive life of dignity in India, now many have reluctantly concluded that it is not even a remote possibility. Some still cling to that hope for a variety of reasons. Human motives are complex, judgement difficult and often faulty.

It has been 45 years since Israel became a reality but even today not every Jew is for Israel. Similarly, not every Sikh may see the argument for an independent Khalistan. But these are questions on which grown men may differ. People also change with time if they have room to grow. I will address the issue of Khalistan elsewhere but using a litmus test of political correctness to determine one's religious commitment is both irrelevant and perverse. If we find fault with the discernment or dedication of Khushwant Singh or General Aurora, let us open our doors to an ongoing dialogue with them and others like them. Both we and they might become the better for it. A political yardstick is entirely inappropriate to determine who is a Sikh.

The second acid test for a Sikh which has come in vogue particularly within the past ten years or so says: Do you as a male Sikh wear the preeminent of the five Sikh symbols — long unshorn hair and a turban? In other words, are you visibly a Sikh? For obvious reasons, this criterion has acquired major importance outside India. The question of who is a Sikh has fueled much debate. Historians like McLeod who take a more scholarly approach have been accused of being selective in their interpretation. Sikh scholars understand the issue but because of their feelings for Sikhism, objectivity may suffer and their analysis become vulnerable. In the process, more heat than light is shed on the subject. I confess to being subjective and will pull in only selected historical events to buttress my view. Why? Because religion is a reality to which the historical intellectual analysis alone is ill-suited. Only in part can history and intellect measure the intuitive reality that transcends both. However, without the selective application of logic and reason, religion is quickly reduced to the levels of dogma and superstition.

The requirement that a Sikh be visibly so has merit. In India, if the small minority of Sikhs opts not to look different from the majority surrounding them, they will quickly lose all independent identity and existence. They will then surely be engulfed by Hinduism and disappear from India just as Buddhism did. The oft-boasted tolerance of Hinduism is a myth which deserves closer scrutiny. If Christianity and Islam found roots in India, it was not because of Hindu tolerance, if any. Political power and patronage supported and nurtured them. Now that the rulers of India are predominantly Hindus, the fate of the Muslims and Christians is the same as that of any other minority such as the Sikhs — harassment and denial of basic rights. The history of how Buddhism was decimated in India is not a kind commentary on Hindu tolerance. St Thomas who took Christianity to India is buried there but, thanks to the Brahmins, he did not die a natural death. How tolerant could Hinduism be of others if it treats almost half of its own believers as untouchables and its women as less than human? One only has to read the Laws of Manu to comprehend the dogmatic inhumanity of Hinduism to its own people. In every religion the followers fall short of the teaching, but in this case, the teaching may be seriously flawed.

I recall that some twenty years ago, neither the President nor the Secretary of our new gurdwara in New York were recognizable Sikhs. They were good people, devoted to the cause and as proof of our tolerance, were elected. At about that time, some new arrivals had problems finding employment; the hiring company insisted that they report to work without their long hair or turbans. After a series of hearings and discussions, we won the point. But the issue was a watershed in our presence here. The opposing lawyer had the temerity to point out that since the senior officers of our gurdwara were without long unshorn hair, this symbol of Sikhism could not be very significant. Needless to say, we were on the defensive, our arguments disjointed and the Indian Consulate in New York least helpful. We were relieved to prevail but it was not a reassuring experience. I think sometime soon thereafter, most gurdwaras in the United States made it a requirement that all office bearers be recognizable Sikhs.

Such a rule, however, opens up a Pandora's box. Now, if the

differences are political or personal, it is easiest to attack a man at his most vulnerable aspect — his Sikh lifestyle. Because someone looks like a Sikh does not automatically turn him into a good one. Some Sikhs drink alcohol even if just a little and only socially. Many do not follow all of the requirements on completing their daily prayers. Others are businessmen with all the attendant temptations. Despite their best intentions, the personal or family life of many falls short of the Sikh ideal. A certain level of recognizable hypocrisy creeps into our lives and chinks (chasms?) appear between the teaching and our practice. After all, we are ordinary Sikhs on the road to becoming better ones but certainly no angels. And our gurdwara elections show how easy it is to attack and destroy a well-intentioned man. The onslaught is always led by assailing a man's commitment to Sikhism and labeling him 'anti-Sikh'. I wonder what that appellation means. Should we even have elections in a gurdwara but how else should we identify people for service to our community? But that is a different matter to be discussed another time, elsewhere.

I look at the Christians. They have over 250 denominations and some, Roman Catholics, for instance, are most reluctant to even admit that the others are Christians nor would they cheerfully intermarry with them. In the early period of Christianity, there were more than one pope, each busy excommunicating the others. In the Jews where there are at least three major denominations, the Conservatives recognize no Reform Jews. Even Hinduism has spawned many sects but Hindus are more tolerant of their own divisions perhaps because their theology is so vague and diffuse. Does time extract such a price from all religions?

I wonder if the young, vibrant religion of the Sikhs is headed the same way. Already, there are signs of sects and denominations within Sikhism although the lines between them are not yet clearly or rigidly drawn. There are important doctrinal differences among some of them; for example, *Namdharis* seek guidance from a living person whom they recognize as Guru; whereas, the larger Sikh community following the directive of Guru Gobind Singh, recognizes the *Guru Granth* as the repository of spiritual authority and the Sikh people speaking collectively as the voice of the Guru in temporal matters. Many Sikhs follow particular spiritual teachers and thus differ from others in minor practices but these idiosyncracies are relatively insignificant. Our religion is young. Will there come a time when we will recognize three different kinds of Sikhs: those who have been confirmed (*Amritdhari*) and have taken final vows to maintain all the requirements of the religion; those who look like Sikhs (*Keshadhari*), maintain long unshorn hair but have not taken the final vows (*Amrit*) of the Sikh lifestyle; and finally those who follow the time-honored tradition of Sikhs who like the Marrano Jews hide their identity, and are labeled *Sehajdhari* in the Sikh tradition? It is hoped that in time the *Sehajdharis* will follow the way of the Khalsa to become recognizable Sikhs just as the *Keshadhari* Sikhs will become more committed to become *Amritdhari* Sikhs. We have had *Sehajdhari* Sikhs as an important part of the Sikh community from the time that the Khalsa began over 300 years ago. Many Sikhs, including some associates and contemporaries of Guru Gobind Singh never opted to receive *Amrit* and become Khalsa, but they were not thought any the less for it. Bhai Nandlal for instance, never became Nand Singh nor did the Guru ask that he should.

We need to look at one more category of Sikh, someone who once was either *Amritdhari* or *Keshadhari* and now, for some reason, is no longer a visibly recognizable Sikh. Such a Sikh will be labeled *patit*. Rarely have the apostate (*patit*) Sikhs had an honorable place in our history; the patriot Bhagat Singh is a notable exception. And that is eminently fair. Sometimes we fail to make the necessary distinction between the *Sehajdhari* and the apostate, but it is critical. I have known apostate (*patit*)

Sikhs resent the fact that though gurdwaras welcome them and accept their services or money, yet will not appoint or elect them to any office nor grant them any honor. I think this is as it should be. The doors of a gurdwara are open to anyone and no one, Sikh or otherwise is barred from service or attendance. However, the visibility of appointive or elective office carries with it a public responsibility with ramifications for the life of the community.

I recall a few telephonic conversations I had with a Sikh young woman some years ago when I was still unmarried. Somebody thought we should know each other and gave me her number, so I called her. She was bright, witty and educated. After a few pleasant chats, she asked me: "Are you a modern Sikh?" I was taken aback. I realized what she wanted to know but I resented the implication that a long-haired *Keshadhari* Sikh was somehow less than modern. My response was unfortunately equally thoughtless: "In the sense that I wear clothes when I go out on the street and know which fork to use at dinner, I guess I am not quite primitive and I operate in this modern world. Precisely what do you want to know?" I hope we will not fall into such a trap of dividing ourselves into modern and not-so-modern Sikhs like that young woman. I also believe that how modern we are is determined by what is inside our heads and not by the length of the hair upon them. I also trust that we will remain charitable towards those who fall short along the way. Already there are gurdwaras that cater primarily to one kind of Sikhs or another. And that is unfortunate for it divides us further.

There is an obvious paradox and not a little hypocrisy when those who are not visibly Sikh or are inconsistent in their lifestyle want representatives who at least look like Sikhs. Though true, it is preferable this way. Ideally, all of us would not only profess virtue but also be virtuous. But that is not likely to happen. In an imperfect world, vice will exist. Better to have a society where vices are at least publicly shunned rather than lauded. This way the gap between teaching and practice persists but an awareness of the ideal and some ongoing efforts towards it also remain. I agree with William Hazlitt that "He who maintains vice in theory has not even the capacity or conception of virtue." It's a choice between a world of conscious hypocrisy or cruel cynicism.

There seems a certain incongruity in a religion that derives its identity from a legislated act of a government — a statute — made into law when the British ruled India. The whole model of the government sanctioned Committee (SGPC) which manages historical gurdwaras deserves a closer look. At the end of his tenure, Guru Gobind Singh bestowed temporal Guruship on the Sikh *Panth*, the nation of disciples. None else but the Sikhs, meeting in mindful prayer and acting in an awareness of their heritage, can make the critical decisions on their identity and their future; no government, not even one of Sikhs should usurp that authority. The Sikhs will remain Sikhs only if what they decide is also consistent with their spiritual legacy and tradition. The Sikhs organized their heritage in a Code of Conduct which reached its final resolution in 1935; that document clearly chronicled how the Sikhs view themselves. And ultimately the definition of a Sikh has to be what the community has resolved.

At the individual level, however, a Sikh is he who claims to be one, however incomplete, unpleasant or unacceptable he may seem to us. Our institutions and gurdwaras have to accept that. There is no hierarchy as in the Roman Catholic Church to dictate otherwise and that is all to the good. Although we all know that the private person may fall short of the ideal and we should remain merciful to private failings, we also perceive that the Sikh identity within the community assumes a public persona which has ramifications for Sikhs everywhere. It is true that nothing unites us more than the love of our religion, and nothing divides us more than the practice of it. The dictates of man are not necessarily the will of God. There is real danger in mistaking the one for the other.

On Gurdwaras as Nurseries

I am a Sikh. The religion was born in Punjab 500 years ago. It took root and flourished in the wheat fields of Punjab in India 10,000 miles away. When I came to the United States, there were hardly any Sikhs in New York, and not more than a handful across the country. There were few gurdwaras. Now over thirty years later, almost every state in this country has a gurdwara, many cities have more than one. On the high holy days, they are so crowded that one has to elbow one's way through the throngs to reach the altar. Thirty years ago, there were so few Sikhs that everybody knew everybody, now there are so many that it is impossible to find a familiar face in the sea of strangers. Thirty years ago, if two Sikhs ran into one another on the street, they went out of the way to greet each other. Now there are so many of us, that we cross the street to avoid another; so many that in our politics we can afford to disagree volubly — without being disagreeable! Yet, the gurdwara remains a source of comfort and solace. It is the repository of our spiritual heritage and a nursery where the saplings of today will find their roots in order to flourish and define our future.

I am also an amateur gardener. Some years ago, I saw a beautiful plant at a friend's house. Its colors were vibrant, the flowers seemed to speak to me, they engulfed me in their aroma. I dearly wanted one like that for my living room. Then it would give me the same pleasure that it gave my friend. The friend was kind and we cut out a part of the plant along with a little of the root, being careful to keep it in soil. We transported it ever so gently to my house where I transplanted it into a pot with new soil. For many days, it needed a baby's care. I watched it grow, I talked to it, I gave it special attention so that it would not dry out. Soon the root took hold. Now it barely needs me except to water it occasionally. Even if I neglect it one week, it does not wilt. It looks lush and happy. When I come home from work, the aroma envelopes me and my tiredness melts away. I am rejuvenated every day.

Some weeks ago, as I sat in the gurdwara listening with half an ear to the program secretary make some humdrum announcement amidst the wailing of infants, several thoughts flooded my mind. A gurdwara should be like a nursery but the existing ones did not feel like it. Have we successfully transplanted the Sikhism of Guru Nanak and Guru Gobind Singh in North American soil? A generation of Sikhs brought the plant from India and lovingly tended it at such great cost. Will the new generation of gardeners be prepared to take over? Is this soil receptive? Does the transplant here need treatment and attention of a different nature? Should our nurseries here be modified to suit the new soil and the different climate? Have the roots taken hold? Are there flowers? Will there be fruit? Is the aroma as hypnotic as ever? Could the plant be more lush, the flowers more colorful and the aroma richer in this new environment?

Raised in India, we became Sikhs more by accident than by design. We were raised in Sikh households, so we became Sikhs. Neither in the family at home, nor in the gurdwara or the school was there much systematic attempt at teaching Sikhism to the young. We learnt primarily by osmosis and some by example. We were raised on a mixture of stories and history, some fact and much fiction, about Sikhism which became an inseparable part of us. The experience of Sikhism became an integral part of our bones, but it was never an intellectual encounter. It is true that the reality which forms the essence of religion transcends the intellect — our senses cannot perceive, our intellects cannot fathom but our souls can commune with this reality. Yet Sikhism keenly appreciates the worth of the intellectual effort and critical reasoning also. Certainly, to many of our young people who are growing up outside the comfortable cocoon of a Sikh community, the intellectual understanding of Sikhism paves the way to a deeper perception.

On the other hand, to many of our first generation immigrants here, a gurdwara is less important for any spiritual solace it may provide and more valuable for the cultural comfort. In the gurdwara, these Sikhs can forget the alien environment with all its frustrations — the problems of work, the social isolation, the emotional exhaustion. The Punjabi Sikh, therefore, tries to recapture and recreate the sights, the sounds and the smells of home. There is nothing wrong with that. In fact, it helps the new arrivals preserve their sanity. Ergo, the religious service becomes most crowded not at its beginning but nearer its end when the socializing begins. The *granthi*, therefore, speaks only in Punjabi; he understands no English for he never speaks to any people who do not speak Punjabi. His congregation is usually more comfortable in Punjabi than any other language and using Punjabi gives them both a sense of home. He never learns about other religions of this society for he never represents Sikhs to the outside world. The community becomes increasingly xenophobic. Such a gurdwara or *granthi* cannot answer the needs of a novitiate but that is what the young Sikhs born and raised outside India are like.

There are other needs of a new community here that a gurdwara could address and accommodate — and needs to. Years ago, when my library on comparative religion and Sikhism was more modest, I eagerly went to the gurdwara to buy or borrow books and found that my measly collection was already far superior, and the gurdwara had no outlet for sale. A Sikh friend who was hospitalized for a few weeks complained that what made him feel worse and most alone was that all other patients but him were visited by their pastors. Why? Because our *granthis* don't know that this would be expected of them. They were never trained to counsel the lonely and the sick, the sexually troubled teenager and the drug addict, or those in the midst of domestic or intercultural conflict. They were never prepared to consider new social issues that impact on their congregation everyday - matters like alcohol and drug addiction, AIDS, racism, sexism, peace and disarmament, environmental crisis and so on. Instead, we argue if it is alright to serve pizza or peanut butter sandwiches for our fellowship meal or *langar*. We get seriously irate over the guitar-strumming young Sikh who sings a ballad in English to the glory of the religion. We are more content to debate Khalistan as if its fate is to be decided by the rising crescendo of our anger, than the myriad of issues that impact on our daily lives.

The new arrival needs to know how this society functions, how to look for a job, a mate or a place to stay. What institutions of this society can help him and how best can he utilize them? What are the rules of social interaction here? Where are the icy patches of behavior in this community where one must tread carefully? He needs a gurdwara which is a spiritual retreat from the battles of life, where he can come to be rejuvenated to fight another day — and how. The young need to know that much as it is possible to be a good Jew and a good American or a good Christian and a good American and so on, similarly it is possible to be a good Sikh and a good American; these are not mutually exclusive ideas. Only then will we carve our rightful and equal niche in the complex and rich mosaic of this society. Where else should he learn all that but in a gurdwara?

The Sikhs need to develop a nursery which can provide a receptive soil to a precious sapling.

Granthi—Priest, Rabbi or Minister?

There are several drawbacks to emigrating and a major gain. One has to recast one's assumptions and cultural framework in terms of the new, host culture and in a new language. Such transformation is not easy. Since culture and language are inseparably intertwined, many of the religious and cultural concepts cannot be adequately or accurately expressed in a different language. Yet, effective communication requires that we try. The constant immersion in a new system and a new society forces us to think afresh our fondest assumptions and beliefs — and that is the gain though it is not without pain.

I smile to myself when I hear a Sikh refer to a gurdwara as our "church" in a non-Sikh gathering. He is trying a short-cut to communication but loses precision in the process. A gurdwara is definitely not a church just as a synagogue is not one, and nor is it a mosque. And now with so many gurdwaras outside India, it is time for the word gurdwara to take its rightful place in the lexicon describing places of worship. What also bothers me is our confusion in how to refer to the person who conducts the religious service in a gurdwara. Is he akin to a priest, a minister, or a rabbi or is he uniquely different? What should we expect of him? What moral or ecclesiastical authority does he have? What title shall we give him when we speak in English so that his position and functions are not misunderstood?

When Guru Nanak settled in Kartarpur after his many travels he became an active farmer. He tilled the lands, earned an honest living, fed his family and preached his message. In many ways, his life remains the ideal. Given the bent and

88

history of the Hindu Brahmin who made a business of religion and sold religious indulgences while making himself the sole proprietor of this less than honest trade, the pragmatic Sikh mind remains skeptical of a professional clergy. At one level we feel that no man should sell religious knowledge; such truth should be freely given and to profit from it would be sinful. Yet we recognize that the person who dedicates his life to learning and teaching about Sikhism needs to be paid. Religious learning is his trade just as you and I making our living from other vocations. And like us, he too has a family to support and bills to meet; the world does not put food on his table. This dichotomy in our thinking does not sit well. The result is that the man who performs the religious service is usually inadequately and grudgingly compensated, and little respected. At another level, however, we also see that this man brings us the teachings of our Gurus and sometimes both the heart and purse strings open most generously. Some itinerant preachers rake in millions.

Our preacher has historically been called a *Bhai* which translates into 'Brother' or *Granthi* which means 'curator of the *Guru Granth*'. '*Granthi*' appears to be a more accurate term and it seems to me that it need not be translated into English. A rabbi is not called someone else in English, nor should he be. An Imam remains that in English as well. Pundit, the Sanskrit word for a scholar is now part of the English language. If non-Sikhs are not now familiar with the word *Granthi*, they will, in time and with usage. Some concepts lose their majesty, power and accuracy upon translation.

The *granthi* is very different from a priest. Sikhism has never recommended, required or taught that a *granthi* be celibate. In fact, most Sikhs would be suspicious and leery of one who was. In the Sikh view, the family life is the right way, renunciation just would not do for either the clergy or the laity. In the Roman Catholic Church, the office of the priest carries certain ecclesiastical authority which is not granted to the clergy by the Sikhs. The office of the *granthi* is accepted by the Sikhs as a necessity. The respect for the man who occupies it does not come with the title; it has to be earned and depends upon the individual. The expositions of the *granthi* are at best recommendations. In many ways, the style of the traditional *granthi* is that of a Talmudic scholar, his sermons and writings are commentaries on Sikh scriptures and he often attempts to apply the lessons of history to contemporary life-situations. He never speaks *ex cathedra*, no matter how important the subject, how strongly he feels about it, or how venerated he is. Anyone may openly disagree with him or engage him in debate, though not while a service is in progress. Also in most gurdwaras, his tenure of office depends upon the pleasure of the congregation and the management committee that is responsible for the physical property and the financial health of the gurdwara.

There are several caveats to these general statements. Many of the historical gurdwaras in India are managed by a legislated India-wide organization called the *Shiromani* Gurdwara Prabandhak Committee (SGPC). In these gurdwaras, *granthis* are appointed, transferred, certified, etc. by a central system of civil service. For these *granthis*, job tenure is not much different from that of a priest or any other bureaucrat, though moral authority still does not come with the territory. Following the times of the Gurus, four major historical gurdwaras acquired a preeminent place in Sikh psyche and have come to be referred to as '*Takhts*' or Thrones (Seats or Centers) of authority. In this century, during the fifties, another was added to make a total of five; the center at *Akal Takht* in Amritsar, which was founded by Guru Hargobind remains the first among equals among these five. The *granthis* of the five centers of authority are appointed by the SGPC and referred to as '*Jathedars*' — literally leaders of '*jathas*' or bands or the community. These five leaders of the community, after collective deliberation, can issue joint directives or commandments to the community, including notification of a rare honor or castigation of an individual for a particularly heinous act. Even they lack any machinery or system for enforcement of their edicts except the social acceptability and respect for their pronouncements within the Sikh community.

If today not many gurdwaras have women *granthis*, it is custom and not canon. A minuscule minority like the Sikhs could not remain free from the influence of the predominant cultures of India — Hinduism and to some extent Islam. In those two, women are not allowed as functionaries in the temple or mosque. Consequently, few Sikh women became *granthis* although many more perform the duties on an informal basis at Sikh services. I was amazed to learn that at one time the management of the Golden Temple would not allow any woman to sing within the inner sanctum, since none had by tradition. In reality, there is no function within the Sikh place of worship or in a Sikh service that is not allowed to a woman. It is well to remember that when Guru Amar Das first organized the widespread Sikhs into 22 diocese, several of those named to head them were women.

Some of the cultural dead baggage that we bring with us was brought home to me about three years ago. A newly established gurdwara in New York was looking for a new *granthi*. Many were interviewed. I recommended a young man in his thirties who was fluent in Punjabi and English. As part of the job interview he gave a sermon. He was good but was not seriously considered because many of the older congregation were uneasy — he was too young to be a spiritual leader. It reminded me that John Kennedy, when told he was too young to be President, made an election promise that he vowed never to break — if elected, he promised never to be that young again. The gurdwara found an excellent but older *granthi* instead.

Guru Gobind Singh is said to have sent several promising

Sikh scholars to various centers of indigenous Indian vedic philosophy. These scholars on their return formed the nucleus for the first *granthis* because they were well versed not only in the teachings of the Gurus but also in the scholarly tradition of the other major religions of India. From such noble beginnings, we seem to have slipped, although there are still some very erudite *granthis*. By and large, most *granthis* today are limited in their education to a knowledge of Sikh, Hindu and Moslem scriptures. Often their familiarity with history is rudimentary and their sermons are overlaid with a strong dose of mythology and folk-tales. Entertaining but confusing, and certainly not satisfying.

The *granthis* are at a particular disadvantage when they follow the migration of Sikhs away from India. They are usually not schooled in any language but Punjabi nor are they equipped to hold any other job. They have never been exposed to the teachings of Judaism or Christianity — the religions of the West. It becomes impossible for them to represent Sikhism outside to non-Sikhs or participate in inter-religious dialogues. Their role becomes increasingly limited. Their congregation acquire sophisticated lifestyles and are exposed to the temptations, successes and the excesses of the new culture. The *granthi* does not venture outside the circle of the gurdwara very much and cannot experience the needs and the frustrations of his congregation. Increasingly, he becomes only marginally relevant to the lives of the Sikhs, particularly the young. Only the older generation weaned on similar teaching in India listens raptly to the *granthi*. Even they do not find him or his message particularly important to their lives but his presence is comforting because it captures the emotional aura of back home. The listeners, particularly the young, tend increasingly to lead schizoid lives.

Lest someone think that I am too strongly condemnatory — and that is certainly not the intent — I merely ask how many

Sikhs, young or old, confide in the *granthi* about personal or familial problems that confront them? And isn't that a major function of the priest, rabbi, minister or *granthi* — to be a sensitive, learned, ear and counsel. The fault lies not in the *granthi* but in how he is perceived and trained, and in the system which has not responded to the changing needs and times. Parenthetically, I should add that some new Sikh academies in India are training a new, refreshing breed of *granthis*, but they are few and far between. Not long ago, when I had to confront my mortality via a two-week hospital stay, I noticed that our *granthi* does not visit the sick or comfort the old and the poor. He was never taught that this is part of the job. The priest and the rabbi do. A minister must minister and so should a *granthi*. The *granthi* needs to get out from the four walls of the gurdwara. He needs to become a friend and a guide. As the person in the gurdwara, the *granthi* has to be the pivot which holds the community together.

I would like to see a *granthi* who can communicate not only in the language of our scriptures but also in the local argot; who can represent us and our religion to others. A man who is at home in the library but also on the golf course and the tennis court. We do not need a recluse for a *granthi* but one who understands life and is paid accordingly; who is not so busy valuing book-learning that he has no time nor skill to live a full life. Like a Talmudic scholar, he can make the teachings of Sikhism come alive to the needs of today and tomorrow. The *granthi* can create an environment and a feeling where one can laugh at the absurdities of the young, hold a seminar where rebellious questioning is not deemed blasphemy, where frank discussions about sex and drugs would not be shocking, yet where the Guru's grace pervades.

The Gurus were very forthright in their comments about the evils of the day—whether *suttee*, caste system, female infanticide or the use of intoxicants, etc. Our *granthi* needs to be equally forthcoming on what the twenty-first century promises to us — from domestic conflict to the environmental crisis; from dowry system to AIDS; from human rights to disarmament and reproductive rights. This does not mean that the *granthi* needs to be an expert and speak authoritatively on all these matters. No one man can. It does mean that the *granthi* has to provide the atmosphere and the direction where these matters can be freely discussed — experts can always be found. Conclusions will rarely emerge, and any that we derive today may be modified tomorrow with changes in our understanding and our circumstances. The discussion in a spiritual ambience will not lead us astray but will enrich us. And who but the *granthi* should provide the lead?

Who else but the *granthi* should steer the religious service in the gurdwara? No one else is as well trained. He should coordinate the program, arrange the appropriate mix of *keertan* and *katha*. He should invite the appropriate singers of the liturgy, performers or lecturers. His opinion should be respectfully sought and heard if a question arises on interpretation of a religious teaching, doctrine, tradition or dogma. The management committee or other elected representatives have a different job; to set policy, to design guidelines within which the functions are held, to manage the property, raise funds, to hire or fire a *granthi* or other employees and so on. The *granthi* remains answerable to the management as I remain responsible to my Dean for my performance at my University, but how I teach my specialty lies outside the Dean's immediate expertise. If a serious disagreement surfaces, a parting of the ways may be necessary, but the Dean is not trained to, nor does he micromanage my teaching. Why should we think that the management committee of a gurdwara, by virtue of having been elected, all of a sudden have acquired the specialized religious knowledge of a *granthi*? It seems hardly reasonable or operationally efficient for the secretary of the management committee to micromanage the daily religious service.

The duties of a modern *granthi* should occupy him longer than the two to four hours a week that he seems to work in most gurdwaras. And he needs to be well rewarded, consistent with his qualifications as a scholar, and the society in which he operates. He needs and deserves our support and respect for he can help us find the way to an inner beauty and truth. He puts us in touch with our spiritual heritage. He is not a gofer, a janitor or a caretaker serving at the whim of a management committee of people who have little knowledge of religion and less serious interest in it. On the other hand, we should not recast our *granthi* into the role of a Brahmin who is called to officiate at a religious ceremony because without him the ceremony may not be valid. Such a view has no place in Sikh teaching. The *granthi* unlike the Brahmin does not hold the keys of heaven in his hot little hands but he can help us discover our own way to unlock the door.

On the Politics of Gurdwaras

It seems to me self-evident that when the belly is full and a sense of dignity prevails, man wants to assert himself. He may want to work with people but not for them. He wants to be heard. He has the ability to sacrifice and to serve others but wants to be led to it, not driven by blows, like cows to pasture. The need to rise above the self is there, the desire has to be awakened from within. In theory, what better institution can possibly exist for such purpose than that of religion, since religion was designed to awaken the higher self.

Guru Gobind Singh asserted that his Khalsa engages in battle every day. The battlefield of the human mind is what he was recommending. I doubt that he would approve of the battles one sees in gurdwaras every day — legal and physical fights, fisticuffs and sometimes the heavy presence of the police. I suppose that these perpetual disagreements are a healthy testament to the fact that the Sikhs are not unconcerned about the management of their religious institutions, but not necessarily an indication of their good sense. Unlike the Roman Catholics, the Sikhs have no administrative hierarchy which can govern without interference from the laity. There is a caveat to this but more about that later. There is no professional clergy. And that is all to the good. I do wish though that we could disagree without being so disagreeable so often.

For the historical gurdwaras across India, there is an India-wide body, mandated by law and formed in 1920. This body, the Shiromani Gurdwara Prabandhak Committee (SGPC) is an elective council which administers these gurdwaras and their property. It also employs *granthis* who serve this body much like priests serve the Vatican. Such a bureaucratic system of civil service however, does not exist for the majority of gurdwaras, smaller and not historical but community based, which are managed and operated by the community or parish in which they are situated. Often these institutions follow the lead of the British-designed SGPC or of other secular democratic institutions and clubs to elect officers and management committees.

Guru Gobind Singh decreed that after him, the line of Gurus in human form would end; the *Guru Granth* now remains the repository of all spiritual knowledge, and the Sikh community acting in mindful prayer has the authority to decide on temporal matters because many issues change with demands of culture or times. It seems clear that no government or civil authority should determine the activities and the future of Sikh religious institutions; only Sikhs joined in an awareness of the Guru have that prerogative. It has always rankled me that in India, the Government dictates when and how elections to the SGPC are held. It is not a compliment to the Sikhs that the premier body which oversees their religious institutions owes its life and existence to a fiat of the government.

For most of us though, SGPC is of only remote and academic interest. Of much more immediate concern are gurdwaras which we have built with our own hard-earned efforts in the past few years in this country. These are the institutions which reflect our sweat, toil and tears, and which we hope to bequeath to our children, though most of these institutions are so far removed from the lives of our young people that I wonder why would they want them, and what would they do with them?

It is inevitable that where there are people, working relationships should form or dissolve as necessary. In working with fellowmen, a sense of competition is inevitable. In secular, business or civic matters, such contention can only benefit society. In religious matters, such rivalry robs the institution of its aura of oneness. How best then to ensure that people have the opportunity to serve and have the incentive to give, while at the same time maintaining the ambience and the atmosphere where one finds brotherhood of man, and not the mentality of a pack of dogs fighting over a bone. Nowhere does the very human tendency to strut as the leader while at the same time remaining, at least outwardly, as one of the pack show more clearly than in the many lodges, clubs, fraternities and religious institutions that we devise for voluntary service to mankind. How should religious institutions, particularly gurdwaras govern themselves?

Of course, we want the management of our gurdwaras to be democratic. We must not deny any Sikh the opportunity to serve, in fact we wish to encourage him. The virtues of democracy are like those of God, motherhood and apple pie — self-evident and beyond reproach. Ergo, there is hardly a gurdwara in this country which does not have annual elections, and hardly any which hasn't had serious disagreements and trouble over their outcome or procedure. It is time to cast a fresh (jaundiced?), different eye at what we do and more importantly, at what we want in the management of a gurdwara.

An important leg of the tripod that forms the philosophic basis of Sikhism is community service. Where else should it start but in the home and the gurdwara? So it is right that unpaid volunteers provide the bulk of the service. Also, in a service oriented, volunteer organization such as a gurdwara, Sikh tradition says that it never behoves anyone to appear too anxious for an office. Sikhs have never liked anyone who did not make a serious attempt to deny or at least hide his political ambition. The Sikhs prefer their leaders to be reluctant brides, somewhat like Nawab Kapur Singh who accepted a title only when it was thrust upon him. Most often our gurdwara leaders are often shy in wanting power; but having tasted it once, are unfortunately even more obdurate in clinging to their offices. More often than not they have to be cajoled into an office but dragged kicking and screaming out of it. It is the latter quality that we don't want. Are elections then the only, or the best, way to ensure and promote a democratic institution in which the workers are largely unpaid volunteers, and where the leaders must at least appear to be most diffident to assume the mantle?

I think that only one kind of election can work in a religious organization and that is the way that a Pope is elected by the Roman Catholic College of Cardinals — the election is by closed ballot, the electors stay secreted until they have achieved unanimous agreement; the election is announced but not the attending controversy. Since the Sikhs do not have a similar hierarchy, such a process is unthinkable for us. (Let me be clear. I am glad we do not have such a hierarchy; it would not be consistent with Sikh teaching.)

As it is, if I have a driving desire to serve the community and become a candidate, I must at some point indicate to people why I am preferable to my rival. No matter how good my opponent, I must promise more or at least clearly draw a distinction between my position and his, even where little or no difference exists. Some lies necessary to the political process must be invented as in any other political campaign. To win I have to polarize the community. Whoever wins, rivalry will remain, lines drawn, and the community divided — until the next election when new lines are drawn. In the words of H.L. Mencken, "In a democracy a good politician is quite as unthinkable as an honest burglar." The electoral process would necessarily taint even a saint.

Years of watching gurdwara politics convinces me that the operating mechanisms most often are accusations and calumny on both sides driven by pride, prejudice and passion, not reason, and certainly not principle. When the dead hand of power politics begins to squeeze the life and spirit out of an institution and the community, alternatives must be considered. I suggest that we can maintain the democratic structure of the gurdwara as also the spirit of service, minus the ambitious infighting.

In a rephrase of the old Kennedy refrain: Don't just see what you can take from the gurdwara; Look at what you can give to it. How else can gurdwaras grow and flourish? To find an answer, let us go to the roots of our religion. The Sikh religion, like some others, expects its followers to tithe. Some Sikhs don't but many follow this injunction faithfully or at least fitfully. Those who do, interpret it most narrowly and usually donate ten percent of their income. But is that what is meant by ten percent? I think that the Guru's definition is different from that of a Hollywood agent claiming his cut. This ten percent means a tenth of your life — of time as well as earnings — or roughly about two and a half hours per day of your being.

I suggest that each parishioner owes some service to the parish that sustains him or her spiritually. It is not a novel idea, many churches reason similarly. By such logic, all adults who are recognizably Sikh and who worship at a particular gurdwara would be enrolled as active members of it. The assumption here is that a person can and will register only in one gurdwara, although the services in the gurdwara remain open to all. Certainly, in these days of computers this should not be too difficult to affirm. I have touched on this matter elsewhere, but I do feel very strongly that those who represent us publicly must be recognizable Sikhs though I realize that outward symbols are no guarantee of a consistent lifestyle. Thus I am willing to forgive private failing from which no one is exempt. But I see that particularly in a non-Sikh ambience, the public persona is important for it has implications for the life of the community. In this matter, therefore, I am accepting of a measure of hypocrisy but not of public cynicism.

The way I see it, from the membership rolls of registered parishioners, gurdwara management committee could be chosen by random preference. It is quite possible that one year we may be saddled with a preponderance of imbeciles but that does not bother me all that much; we have survived stupidity, incompetence as well as criminality before. Also, there is a way to minimize at least the effects of possible inadequacy or inexperience; have the previous year's officers serve as a committee of advisers to the present committee and also select a slate of officers-elect who will assume office next year when the present committee in turn become advisers. This will insure that continuity in policy is maintained. It will also mean that new people who will not normally enter gurdwara management will get a chance to serve. It will produce a system of training and will impart managerial skills to our members — skills that are also useful elsewhere.

There are ancillary benefits to such a model which drafts people by lottery. No man who is selected an officer can go around puffing his chest and claiming to be a community leader (he is at best a community representative), because his office is a gift from the community (*sangat*) attained by grace of the Guru and in no way a reflection of his popularity or competence. It is truly an appointment to serve, not an office to harangue or lord over the people. It is not earned but granted by the congregation (*sangat*). The sangat remains paramount. Guru Gobind Singh proved it by requesting his followers to baptize him, and by clearly assigning all the glory for his success to his followers.

I also think it would be better if the titles used for various offices are not the usual ones of Director, President and so on, for they speak of power and of a man on an ego trip. Simpler titles indicative of the Sikh concept of service, preferably in Punjabi would be better. (Quite obviously, titles in Punjabi would be novel to most, but even the non-Sikhs, non-Punjabis will learn given the opportunity.) I realize that sometimes a particular person may not be able to serve for personal or professional reasons; an exemption may then be granted upon presentation of sufficient cause. The concept is not much different from the one that requires each citizen to be available for jury duty unless excused for good reason. There are duties and rights to being a Sikh as there are to being a citizen of a country.

It is not commonly seen in the gurdwara committees that I have observed, but there are two principles they need to keep in mind in their meetings. They need to remind themselves that they are a religious body, meeting for a cause that transcends the self, so their meetings should begin and end in mindful prayer — perhaps then the middle would not be so dreary. And they need to get acquainted with Robert's Rules of Order. I would strongly suggest that the management committee of a gurdwara should manage the physical facilities, finances, hiring and firing of personnel including the *granthi*, and in the general design of policy, but stay out of the religious instruction and programs. It is disturbing if not insulting to have members of the committee micromanaging a religious function for most of them have neither the skill nor the interest. Religious programming is rightly the bailiwick and expertise of the *granthi* and he should design that portion according to the guidelines provided by the committee. Even when the committee meets, unless the issue pertains to the *granthi* himself, he should be present as an *ex officio* member to ensure that whatever is discussed or decided is consistent with Sikh teaching and tradition. The *granthi* is a scholar of the Sikh religion and needs to be recognized as such. Much like the army in a democracy which remains answerable to the elected government of civilians, the *granthi*, however, must remain answerable to the management board which is composed of the laity.

I also suggest that the far-flung corners of our community need to be knit, not into a monolithic organization, but into a cooperating network of autonomous units. Each gurdwara with a parish exceeding, say 50 adults, could nominate one member to a Central Sikh Council for the United States; the term for each nominee could run, say, three or four years. This Council could speak for Sikhs at the national or international levels, perhaps issue a quarterly journal, publish relevant books, sponsor events or symposia, and in general be an umbrella organization which can respond in a more powerful and meaningful way as and when needed. To give an example, during the Reagan years we lost the right to serve as recognizable Sikhs in the armed services of the United States. What other body but a Central Sikh Council should lead the struggle on a national scale to restore these rights? Our gurdwaras across the country have taken on several meritorious projects for community service such as feeding the homeless, providing medical screenings and organizing blood drives. Such a Council can put us on the national and international maps for such activities. Let the minimum expenses of such a Council be met by nominal assessments from the member gurdwaras (units), say $500 per year.

No matter how well intentioned the people, sometimes differences will occur. Several procedures could help. A primary constitutional requirement of any gurdwara would have to be that officers (*sevadars*) would hold office for only one term and would not be eligible for reselection for at least one term. Any disputes that cannot be resolved locally would be referred to the Central Council for binding arbitration or adjudication. The Council would have a standing Rota, Tribunal or Judicial Bench of perhaps five members who would weigh the evidence and arbitrate or otherwise resolve issues that come before it. Since we are dealing with a religious institution, I believe it necessary that two or three members of the Bench be *granthis*. In doctrinal matters, a tribunal of *granthis* is more meaningful. Obviously a member of the Bench would disqualify himself if the case comes from his jurisdiction. It doesn't have to be what

I suggest, but I believe it important that we design some such model of ecclesiastical authority so that our gurdwaras stop running to the civil courts of the land every other day , as they now seem to. By such behavior, we abrogate our responsibility and, in a sense, hand our affairs to others, making them the custodians of our destiny.

I realize that what I propose is a radical departure from what exists. But I assure you, one has to be a veteran of the gurdwara election wars or at least have witnessed some, to appreciate why an alternative to elections is imperative. Words cannot convey their brutality. Lest it seem too much like sour grapes, I confess that in the past I have held elective offices in the gurdwara and appointive offices in gurdwara committees and other Sikh organizations. I speak today from a sense of self developed over years of service in academia that I am one of life's lone furrowers and do not plow well when yoked to elephantine, multimember committees except briefly and in small doses. So now I usually shy away from gurdwara management except in special projects.

One needs to remember that ultimately our effectiveness and impact will be determined not by the shrillness of our rhetoric but by the quiet measured force of our reason. As Eugene McCarthy said, "Being in politics is like being a football coach. You have to be smart enough to understand the game and stupid enough to think it's important."

Religion and Politics - What a Mix!

Over the past ten years or so, particularly since the Indian Army entered the Golden Temple in 1984, the Indian Government spokespersons have repeatedly tried to promote the argument that gurdwaras should be restricted to worship and prayer; no political issues should be discussed there, for such matters demean the sanctity of holy places. Jawahar Lal Nehru, the first Prime Minister of free India, lucidly articulated the concept that the mix of religions and politics was an explosive one. Since the rise of Ayatollah Khomeni in Iran and the tide of Islamic fundamentalism, the world has rightly become wary of such a blend. Though not as widely noted, the rise of Hindu chauvinism in India is equally pernicious; notice the Hindu determination to destroy the 500-years-old Babri mosque and replace it with a Hindu temple. Nehru's daughter, Indira Gandhi, the former Indian Prime Minister, pushed the idea more forcefully and globally in order to weaken the Sikhs at home and malign them worldwide for mixing politics and religion. The litany has been artfully continued and elaborated by her followers, including Zail Singh, the former President of India. Many Sikhs have come to join such a chorus; either they do not understand its implications or find themselves to be too much on the defensive. On the other hand, some Sikhs have vociferously maintained their traditional right of being able to discuss political matters within gurdwaras but have looked at such a practice as being unique to the Sikh religion. Asking for any such special privilege for the Sikhs is wrong and begs the question.

On the surface, the Indian Government's position sounds

entirely logical and absolutely unassailable but believe me, it is absurd. When Bishop Desmond Tutu led a moral movement for political change in South Africa from his church, nobody found it wrong. When Martin Luther King led a powerful nationwide crusade against racism from his church, nobody accused him of sinfully mixing politics and religion. His chant of "We shall overcome" was not perceived to be politically threatening to the established government. When we daily beseech the Roman Catholic Church to be more active in movements for empowerment of people and for social and political change in Latin America, it is because we know that to be a primary function of a religion. Are birth control, abortion rights and freedom of choice strictly religious and personal matters or are they to be decided in the political arena alone? Is it possible to separate the two entirely and completely? Look at how these issues have dominated and claimed the political agenda in the United States, look at their importance in impoverished Roman Catholic nations in Latin America. Their socio-economic impact is clear. How can such moral, ethical and religious elements be divorced from political programs?

If the White House is the bully pulpit for the President to articulate his societal vision, religion provides a different pulpit to integrate the internal and the external parts of the self. Even the most cursory look at history will tell us that social conscience is forged by religion, social policy is hammered out in the heat of political debate.

Bishop Tutu and Reverend King received Nobel Prizes and honors all over the world for their efforts, not abuse and calumny for mixing politics and religion as has been the fate of Sikh leaders. When Mahatma Gandhi (though his achievements were all in the political arena, '*Mahatma*' is an honorific based in religion, not politics) led India's movement for freedom from the British, he issued most of his policy directives or political statements following a prayer meeting ; the press would meet him there. If that was not wrong, why is it wrong for the Sikhs to start a political agitation after a prayer meeting?

When we ask that religion and state remain separate, we mean something else. A policy of separation of religion and government makes sense but one must understand what that concept means. Government should be blind to religion. We are citizens — not atheist citizens, Jewish citizens, Christian citizens of a particular denomination, or Sikh citizens. It is not right to ask that a citizen should have to affirm "So help me God" though most will not mind. An affirmation of honor and an awareness of the laws against perjury should be necessary in court or at being sworn into office, not an oath. Some states in this country, like California, allow such an affirmation, but most states still do not. I am sure Jefferson would be disappointed by the statement "In God we trust" on our currency. It does little but to trivialize both God and man. It is well to remember that this inscription on our currency dates only from the 1950s as do the words "one nation under God" in the Pledge of Allegiance. The essence of the First Amendment is two-fold: one says there will be no establishment of religion by the state and the second refers to free exercise of religion as a fundamental right of citizens. These two clauses are interdependent; the latter cannot exist without the state honoring the former.

The concept of separation of church and state means only one thing: the state shall not establish a religion. A corollary is that the state will not endorse or aid any particular religion nor would it hinder any. It means that the resource or might of a government is not to be used in matters of religion. It emphatically does not mean that religious people will not enter politics, nor that politicians would have no religion. It does not mean that politicians will not discuss religious matters or that religious people will not debate political issues. It does not mean that laws or political statutes will not be talked about in churches and temples.

If man has any inalienable rights, where else shall he talk about them except in a house of God from whom all such rights flow? If political systems serve to organize and systematize human rights and human obligations to the state, where else should such political institutions be analyzed except in churches, temples, mosques and gurdwaras? Religions need not dictate to man every aspect of his personal and social behavior but they should provide a forum for discussion of all moral and ethical issues — each and every aspect of human activity. Religions should do more than prate empty nonsense about an Infinite God or of a fanciful or feared hereafter. Religions must define man's place in society, his relationship to fellow man. They must make the moral man into a more ethical being. If the men who govern other men must remain unaware of religion, then those who rule us will have no ethics. If a religion makes a man better, we need not less but more religious men in government — men who love their own religion and, at the same time, can also rejoice in another who loves his own equally though differently.

The present dilemma of the Sikhs on mixing religion and politics, particularly in India, is indeed ironic. In the 1920s, when the Sikhs launched a massive nonviolent struggle against the British, finally forcing the British to surrender the keys of the Golden Temple to them, the first man to congratulate the Sikhs was Mahatma Gandhi. He said: "The Sikhs have won the first battle in the struggle for India's independence." His protégé, Nehru also personally visited the Sikhs to felicitate them. Until 1947, Sikhs repeatedly initiated massive movements for India's freedom from the ramparts of the gurdwaras. Neither the British nor the Indian political leaders found such activity a misuse of the holy premises. It was only an independent India (since 1947) which found the Sikh agitations for dignity, human rights and for a respectable framework in free India inappropriate to religious places. The reason is simple.

Now the Sikhs were agitating against these governments of independent India of which they were a part.

When Indira Gandhi suspended India's Constitution in the 1970s and ruled by administrative fiat, the Sikhs launched a historic agitation from their gurdwaras for restoration of democratic rights. Indira Gandhi never forgave them for challenging her. When in 1982 they launched another agitation from the Golden Temple to redefine state rights within India's Constitutional framework, Indira Gandhi resolved to crush them. She realized that their strength flows from their religion and the gurdwaras. Her attempts to divorce religion from political issues were a ploy to sap the energy of the Sikhs which had become so inconvenient, even threatening. That is why the structure and the functioning of the Shiromani Gurdwara Prabandhak Committee (SGPC) flabbergasts me — the Government (at one time British, now Indian) is the parent and the midwife of this strange animal in Sikh politics; it functions at governmental pleasure and by governmental fiat, thus reflecting a pernicious state interference in religious matters.

For years, both Mahatma Gandhi and Nehru appeared at many Sikh gatherings in gurdwaras to seek their support on political issues, as did Indira Gandhi when she ruled India. Many gurdwaras worldwide honored them for their 'political vision' and they accepted such honors gratefully. For Nehru and his descendants, 'separation of politics from religion' was never a matter of principle but is now one of political expediency.

The essence of Sikh teaching has been to mold a man into a 'complete' man; one who loves his own religion but is also equally respectful and tolerant of another who follows his own faith and a different road. Sikhism emphasizes integration of the internal life with the external reality of society. The primary activity of the Sikh religion has been directed at empowerment of those who had been powerless for centuries under the

Muslims and in the Hindu caste system. Guru Nanak spoke of the evils of his day just as much and just as boldly as he spoke of his love of God and the virtues of meditation. There can be no love of God where there is no love of truth and no hunger for justice. The lives of Gurus Arjan, Hargobind, Tegh Bahadur and Gobind Singh particularly emphasize that a dichotomy between religious and secular concerns is false. Of the ten Commandments in Christianity, fully seven refer to man's relationship to man and are best termed elements of social behavior.

If religious institutions do not respond to political issues that affect the lives of their people, those religions would become irrelevant to the lives of the people, and they should. They would no longer remain living religions but become empty shells of meaningless ritual and dogma. Religions must answer man's needs here and now and help relieve his hell in this life rather than promise him a heaven in the hereafter. Heavenly reward for earthly misery is a poor bargain.

Khalistan: One Sikh's View

In writing this, the usual reason — to convey a point of view — is reinforced by a better one, to initiate a debate. Debating Khalistan is an impossible assignment and an unpleasant chore in some ways. Yet it is only in debate that we hone our skills, sharpen our focus and define our goals. And we should not be afraid to take on sacred cows. This discussion is particularly timely because in recent years a litmus test of political correctness has emerged by which to judge a Sikh. If your opinions fall even a hair short of total support for the idea of Khalistan, you are quickly branded anti-Sikh. And this is unfortunate. This debate needs a devil's advocate for an impossible cause and I am that — a devil's advocate.

The word 'Khalistan' conjures some very disturbing images among Indians; people still remember the painful birth of Pakistan. The Indian Government has used the recent demand for Khalistan by Sikhs for some petty and inane policies which are more likely to make that dream of many come true. Many nasty suggestions have been made regarding the Sikhs (send them to Pakistan!) by many Hindus, including Rajiv Gandhi. The reality is somewhat more complex.

Certainly the Sikhs need no lessons in patriotism. It has been repeatedly and clearly established that during the struggle for India's independence, the sacrifice of the Sikhs was far in excess of their proportion in the country; fully 70 to 80 percent of all freedom fighters who were arrested, sentenced, exiled or hanged by the British were Sikhs. Within a few years of Independence, Sikhs had transformed the Punjab into the richest province of India with the highest standard of living. Where India used to have famines every year, now thanks to the Punjabi Sikh farmers, the country can even export food. In many ways, India owes its unity and integrity to the Sikh soldiers who served it so well in its three wars against Pakistan and one against China. How is it that things have changed so much so soon?

Before the attack on the Golden Temple in June 1984 on Guru Arjan's martyrdom day, one could perhaps count on the fingers of one's hand the number of Sikhs who would opt for an independent sovereign republic of Khalistan. After the killings of Sikhs in November, 1984 and the subsequent repressive policies of the Indian Government directed solely against the Sikhs, one can count on the fingers of one's hand the number of Sikhs who would not choose Khalistan. This striking shift occurred within months of the attack on the Golden Temple. Rather than being angry at it, frustrated by it or afraid of it, one should understand that such dramatic swings are not to be taken lightly but are not necessarily etched in stone either. The longer such feelings last, the more entrenched they become and harder to dislodge. The rubicon may well have been crossed in this matter. The massive increase in the demand for Khalistan indicates that the Sikhs are not sure of their place in India. When the present is slippery, the future appears menacing.

Blaming a foreign hand as Indira and Rajiv Gandhi often did is escaping responsibility; an objective view would be more useful. Pakistan has been consistently accused of fomenting and fanning rebellion in Punjab and Kashmir. Not that there is much proof of it but even if it were true, an outsider can only exploit a house divided where discord already exits. If people who have sacrificed so much for the unity, integrity and viability of India for so long now no longer want to be a part of it, there are only two possible explanations. Either most of the 15 million Sikhs were struck by lightning and have lost all reason or there is merit in what they say; one must look at what the Indian Government has promised or delivered to them in the past 45 years.

The Sikhs have long said that the promises made to them by Mahatma Gandhi and Jawahar Lal Nehru before 1947 have not been honored. It was for this reason that the Sikh members of the Constituent Assembly of independent India did not initial their acceptance of the Constitution of India. The record of documents and speeches exists and is simple enough to verify. To have to wait and agitate for 45 years for promises to be fulfilled is indeed to have to wait too long. By now all promises should have been dealt with — fulfilled or negotiated, but resolved. At this time, most Sikhs feel that in India, justice is selective and politics reign supreme. Again, important here is not only the reality but also its perception. To dismiss this feeling as mere hallucination (of 15 million people?) would be compounding an injustice with stupidity.

When Sikhs look at the 500 years of their history, it surprises them that anyone should question their loyalty or their right to live with dignity on their own terms in India. In spite of long-standing disaffection with the Indian Government, the Sikhs' loyalty was not questioned when they defended India against China or Pakistan, nor was it in doubt when Punjab contributed to India's independence or economic recovery. In essence, today's Sikh is saying: "My loyalty to the country is a matter of history; to ask me to take a loyalty oath is an insult. I do not have to prove my fitness for a place of dignity here. You, who have done me wrong and are in such a larger majority than I, have to show me that you wish me to remain a part of India." To whom is this addressed? To the Indian Government and the majority community.

It is necessary to remember that despite the attack on the Golden Temple and the widespread state terrorism directed specifically against them, Sikhs did not rebel *en masse* from

India. Examine this behavior of the Sikhs in the context of what Lincoln said at his first inaugural in 1861: "If by the mere force of numbers a majority should deprive a minority of any clearly written constitutional right, it might, in any moral point of view, justify revolution ..." Indira Gandhi, who probably wanted a strong united India, will be remembered as the one who fragmented the people and dismembered the country.

If the Indian Government cannot act swiftly, decisively and effectively to assure the Sikhs of justice and security, it will never regain its right to govern nor should it. The Sikhs then would have little choice but to carve out a homeland of their own. Khalistan, no matter how small or imperfect, would then become a reality. Demands of human dignity will prevail and, be it ever so humble, be it ever so meager, Khalistan will also exist among the nations of the world. No army and no governmental rhetoric will be able to prevent it. And at this time the Indian Government has clearly lost any claims to the hearts and minds of the Sikhs. I submit to you that the conventional arguments why Khalistan is not viable are nonsense. That the country would be small or landlocked and its economic base limited — these things do not matter. The country would be larger than many member states of the United Nations, its economy better than that of many emerging nations in Eastern Europe.

In recent years, many Sikhs have presented most lucidly all the good arguments for Khalistan — the broken promises, systematic injustice to the Sikhs, all the history, etc. But as T.S. Eliot reminds us, "History has many cunning passages, contrived corridors and issues, deceives with whispering ambitions. Guides us by vanities." The issue of Khalistan is not all black or white. It is not Khalistan now or Khalistan never; it is perplexing.

I can present several good reasons why Khalistan is not desirable. Never in their history have Sikhs set about to conquer territory, subjugate people in the name of religion or establish Sikhism as state religion. Ranjit Singh, for instance, was a ruler who happened to be a Sikh and not a particularly good one at that; in his later years, he was much better at being a ruler. He did not establish Sikhism as the state religion. His administration was secular. His Punjab remained a multireligious country. It did not became a Sikh Punjab.

Let us look at it somewhat differently. I am a minority no matter where I live — in India or wherever. When I came here in 1960, there were two Sikhs in New York; in Oregon where I went to school, I was the only one. Many of you can share that experience. Except in Punjab, even in India I remain a minuscule minority. A part of me says, wouldn't it be nice, wouldn't it be right if there was little bit of dirt, a little part of this earth which was mine, where I was the king! And that says — Khalistan now. Another part of me says where I hold sway, there will be someone else — a non-Sikh — who will not, whose sensitivities will be ignored, whose rights will be a little abridged, who will not be the chosen one, who will be second class for no fault except that he is not a Sikh. And that is not the Sikh way. That says to me that countries based on religious identity alone are not desirable. Two examples that come to mind are Pakistan and Israel.

But what is undesirable can become historically necessary and even inevitable. Again Pakistan and Israel come to mind. Two thousand years of diaspora, bigotry, suffering and pogroms convinced the Jews and the world of the necessity and the inevitability of a Jewish homeland. Before the formation of Pakistan in 1947, the demand was not a longstanding one. Just before India's independence, Mahatma Gandhi and three others dominated the political scene — Nehru, Patel and Azad. Nehru — the father of Indira Gandhi became the Prime Minister, Patel was the Home Minister, and Azad — the sole Muslim, others were Hindus - was the Education Minister. Azad wrote his diaries which were sealed for a number of years after his death and finally opened a couple of years ago. In them, he put the blame for Pakistan squarely on Nehru. He claimed that Nehru and his Hindu dominated political party was most reluctant to share power with the Muslims and the Muslims were suspicious of the Hindus. Result: a partition of the country and Pakistan became not only necessary but inevitable. Seems like history may be repeating itself in Punjab.

The partition of the country in 1947 carried a horrendous price tag. Nations are formed when there is a shared culture, language, history and so on, not necessarily religion only. The shephardic and ashkenazy Jews in Israel do not get along all that well even though both are Jews. Religion alone could not hold together Pakistan and Eastern Bengal, now Bangladesh. Someday I am sure, Bangladesh and Indian Bengal would want to come together as Greater Bengal, based not on religion but on culture, as can be seen in the reunification of Germany. The demand for Khalistan has to be looked at in perspective. Before 1984, no responsible Sikh leader demanded Khalistan with one exception: Jagjit Singh Chauhan who is London-based and has been asking for Khalistan for over 20 years. I met him in the seventies and he was a voice in the wilderness, not many gurdwaras would give him the time of day. In 1984, Bhindranwale did not plant a flag and declare, "No more India, we are Khalistan — a separate, sovereign country" although there was sufficient provocation, nor did any other Sikh leader.

When Pakistan was formed, the Sikhs suffered — we lost a lot. The refugee problem was worse than in Europe after the Second World War. The lives lost! We also lost a part of our heritage. The birthplace of Guru Nanak, the historical places in Lahore and Punja Sahib, to name a few. If Khalistan were to be carved today, we would lose a lot more of our inheritance. The Gurus did not live and preach only in Punjab. They travelled all over India from Assam and Bengal to the South. More importantly, look at our people. The Sikhs are an outgoing, assertive, outward-looking people. They would not be satisfied for long, hemmed in a minicountry with limited opportunities. Soon the borders would be strained. Pakistan is friendly now but for how long? Remember only people and individuals have friendships, nations do not; they have only self-interest to guide them. The words Pakistan and Khalistan literally mean the same — "land of the pure" in their respective languages. How neighborly will be two lands of the pure and for how long?

If Khalistan is undesirable, has it become necessary and inevitable? Now that the demand for Khalistan has surfaced, how hard a demand is it? Is it written in stone? I am not sure, even though I realize that once the genie is out of the bottle, it is difficult if not impossible to push it back.

Despite all the injustice to the Sikhs, in 1985 Longowal and the Sikhs signed an accord with the Indian Government — to give peace another chance. Too bad that the Indian Government of Rajiv Gandhi did what Indira Gandhi had done earlier: they did not fulfill their promises but delivered more repression. Again, in 1989, the Sikhs participated in the electoral process, won by landslides, welcomed the new Prime Minister V.P. Singh into a peaceful, open Punjab — no security was necessary. By this act—they clearly showed the world that they were not rejecting ties to India, only that the nature of the ties had to change. Until only one year ago, Simranjit Singh Mann was still looking for a solution within the Indian constitutional framework. Too bad that the Government delivered what it always did — more repression.

Nations cannot be bonded by force as the Soviets have discovered, but only by enlightened self-interest. The West Europeans are learning that closer political and economic ties can be beneficial to all — of course there is resistance because of the history of centuries of suspicion, war and bloodshed. It can't be easy for any of the Europeans to comfortably trust the Germans. If the Soviets had disbanded earlier, a looser, cooperating confederation of nations might have resulted — now the Ukrainians, the Lithuanians and the Estonians are at each other's throat. Just look at Yugoslavia. India awaits a similar fate and needs enlightened leadership.

I can visualize the whole Indian subcontinent - including Pakistan and Bangladesh — remarcated into several secular nation-states based on culture, language and economic interest; the level of cooperation to be determined by their self-interest and their shared history. As it is, I find that most of us Sikhs have more in common with the culture of Punjab and that means Pakistan than with the rest of India where I can only communicate in English. In post-Independence India, the only cultural phenomenon that may be the uniting glue of modern India appears to be the Hindi movie industry; any nation deserves better. I would like to see the nation-states free to pursue their own economic and cultural development and not be under the heels of remote bureaucrats in Delhi. Only then will they be able to preserve their rich heritage and contribute to the diversity and richness of the Indian subcontinent.

To my mind the Sikhs have clearly rejected the model of the present Indian governing system. Khalistan though undesirable has become increasingly necessary, primarily because of the shortsighted policies of the Indian Government. Has it become inevitable?

By now events have probably already overtaken what I have written here, but when I look at my views, I have to echo Walt Whitman who said, "Do I contradict myself?. Very well then I contradict myself. (I am large, I contain multitudes.)" The issue of Khalistan can and should be debated but it will eventually be decided not in New York, London or New Delhi but in the streets and villages of Punjab. In the meantime, Sikhs everywhere support the legitimate aspirations of our people in the Punjab in whatever form they are expressed. One thinks of Jefferson who said, "I weep for my country when I reflect that God is just."

Identity and Integration:
At the Crossroads

This happened five or six years ago. A group of new immigrants, primarily Asians, decided to hold a parade in the streets of New York to celebrate, showcase and highlight the diversity of New York. The organizing committee was understandably dominated by new immigrants from China, Korea, Philippines, India and Pakistan since these are the new Americans. The Mayor, perhaps even the Governor, might attend. What better way for our neighbors to learn about us. So far so good.

Problems soon surfaced, particularly with the Indians in the group. They wanted to parade as they would in India. They wanted a reviewing stand, with a politician from India on it, failing that, an Indian filmstar or at least the Indian Ambassador or the Consul General. It would make good copy back home and a great opportunity for being seen and photographed with the people considered important, particularly in India. They also insisted that all immigrants of Indian descent march behind the flag of India.

At this all hell broke loose. Since this was after the invasion of the Golden Temple in 1984 by the Indian Army, most Sikhs were reluctant to give any recognition to a symbol of India or to any representatives of its Government. Most Muslims and Kashmiris were similarly disposed, being equally bitter with the Indian Government. The Sikhs wanted to march, but leading them would be the saffron flag of the Sikhs. Most Hindus however, were adamant; if you refused to honor the Indian politicians or march under the Indian flag, that was *prima facie*

119

evidence that you were a traitor to India. Unwisely, the Indian Consul General stuck his nose where it did not belong. The consular officials started coming to the organizational meetings of the Indian contingent. Quickly, at their instigation, passions were aroused, the Sikhs and Muslims were branded unpatriotic and anti-Indian. The Indian Government officials fueled the fire but nobody asked if it was right for them to interfere in the internal affairs of these people, many of whom were no longer citizens of India. The largely Hindu Indian immigrant throng, true to the Indian cultural proclivity for obsequiousness, catered to the controlling influence of the consular officials.

I had been in America over a quarter of a century by then and my ties to the old country were not all that strong. I had been watching the imbroglio with cool amusement and calm detachment, quite sure that it wasn't going to become my problem. Oddly, the same night I got telephone calls from both Hindus and Sikhs soliciting my opinion and support for their respective positions. That set me thinking.

India, like the United States, is a political entity. It seems to me, therefore, that the only political flag that should be displayed on the streets of an American city would be that of this country. I recognize that when a head of state of another country is visiting, the flag of that country would be displayed. But those are special circumstances. My political loyalty and identification is now American, not Indian, though culturally my roots remain Indian. I could love India's cuisine, its music and philosophy, even its people, yet I vote here, not in India. To visit India, I need special permission in the form of a visa from the Indian Government, just like any other non-Indian. And that permission may be denied by some functionary of the Indian Government without reason, as happens often enough to enough people.

The United States is a diverse country, a mosaic of the many cultures that have come here. In fact, this country's vitality and strength flow from its diversity. I can see a celebration of that diversity. I can see groups marching behind the banners of their cultural, religious or even geographic affiliations, but not those of political entities.

My views are further strengthened when I think about many of the other immigrants who have stronger differences with the governments of their native countries. Under what banner would the Cuban immigrants march? Certainly not that of the present-day Cuba exemplified by Castro. The aegis of the deposed Batista's people would be equally repugnant and out of the question. Would Palestinians from the occupied territories agree to march as Israelis with an Israeli politician on the reviewing stand? When this incident happened, East Germany was a separate country and the Soviet Union was the big bad wolf. What would happen to immigrants from those countries? The list is endless.

One has to remember that many immigrants who chose America did so out of political necessity. They were survivors, victims of their own governments; whereas many Indians had come here in search of the economic pot of gold. (In the past five years or so, many Sikhs have left India to escape that government's repressive policies and torture and have been granted political asylum here.) In addition, there are Sikhs who were born and raised in Burma, Kenya, Great Britain or this country. Many of them have never been to India. They feel no kinship with India the political entity, but can and do relate to that culture, music, language and cuisine to a varying extent. Certainly, they cannot identify with the flag of India, but only with its religious and cultural organizations.

It seems to me self-evident that under no circumstances should the representatives of the erstwhile country of an immigrant group be welcome either at the organizational stage or later during the parade on a reviewing stand. They could, if they wish, take their place along with the crowds we all hoped would be there.

That was my logic and I proclaimed it clearly and publicly. The hate mail from my Hindu friends surprised me. One Hindu colleague stopped speaking to me and did not resume amicable conversation until three years later. One Hindu patient and his family walked out of my office, to return a month later. Unknown Indian-accented voices left obscene messages on my answering machine. This was not new to me — I had seen it after I said some frank things at Indira Gandhi's assassination. But it hurt, nevertheless.

Finally came the icing on the cake. A kind friend arranged a dinner meeting with the Indian Consul General. I had no problem with that. There were four of us Sikhs — professors of Mathematics and of English, a physician and myself — to engage the Consul General in a discussion. I remember that the food was excellent, the discussion a disaster. I cannot imagine a more confined and limited mind than that of the Consul. I could not help but pity India — a country so richly endowed in nature and talent and so poorly served by its bureaucrats and politicians.

The Consul was of one fixed mind — all Sikhs, no matter where they were born and raised, or whatever their political loyalty, affiliation or feeling, must march behind the flag of India. According to him, for Sikhs to display the flag of their religion in New York in preference to that of India would be a gross insult to India. It would be high treason. At the most, he could allow both the Indian and the Sikh flags as long as we observed that, in his words, "A country's political flag must outrank that of a religion and must fly higher, or be ahead in a procession." We reminded him that the Sikh flag had been at the head of many processions in India, and many Indian politicians had marched behind it and there was no national flag alongside or ahead of it. In the forty years that India had been independent, no government had propounded the view that the Sikh flag was unacceptable. The more we talked, the angrier he became. He was an observing Christian. Finally in desperation, I suggested that the next time he was in St. Patrick's Cathedral he should look up and notice if he saw one flag or two, and if that of the Church was any lower than that of the State. The result was not quite what we expected. He sputtered, turned all shades of the spectrum, pronounced the meeting useless and ended it.

It is many years now and many a Consul General have come and gone, but I still wonder about the incident.

We who come from India remain primarily Indian in outlook and in many parts of our being, even though we change in many ways and live here for the better part of a lifetime. This is not so unusual in first-generation immigrants no matter where they come from. The cultural affinities are in the marrow of our bones, not easily shattered, nor is there any reason that they should. As I said, the richness of this country depends upon the ideas and the heritage that we and other immigrants like us have brought. Our children will have more of the American cultural traditions grafted onto their Indian roots than us, and this process will continue unabated from generation to generation. Every new generation of immigrants has brought a rich heritage which has found a unique niche, however small, in the complex mosaic of this society such that the whole is greater than the sum of the parts.

When I look at our new immigrant Sikhs here, I reckon that in some things we need to define more common ground with others from India and Pakistan, particularly when it comes to matters like language, cuisine and music. In matters concerning religion, most of my cohorts are from India, though not all. In issues involving housing and employment, we need to construct working relationships not only with those from the Indian subcontinent but also other Asians and generally with people from all third world nations. In other matters like recruitment into the U.S. armed services and in some job situations as well, we share a commonality of interest more with the orthodox Jews who wear a yarmulke than with any group from India. In fact, in these matters, the representatives of the Indian Government and Indian groups are often the least understanding or supportive of the Sikhs.

To me, being a good Sikh and a good American are not mutually exclusive concepts. Moreover, one can love the heritage of India of which we are proud products, and yet not identify all that much with the bureaucracy and the Government of India. Identity and integration are not mutually exclusive ideas. Integration is possible only when there is a sense of identity. To become an attractive mosaic requires that each element of the mosaic have a clearly defined niche; only then can the whole be greater than the sum of the parts. To live here and strive to remain unchanged is foolish for it only creates a self-imposed ghetto of the mind. To refuse to change means a refusal to grow. On the other hand, we have brought a rich heritage here; to abandon it is to diminish ourselves and to rob this society as well. By contributing our culture to this mosaic, we pay back for the opportunities it has given us. But that rich heritage of ours does not lie in homage to two-bit politicians or to celluloid gods and goddesses of the Indian film industry. The only desirable integration for a small minority such as ours lies in a mosaic where our identity is sacrosanct.

Dissent and Prior Restraint

Originally I had titled this piece very simply — ?. Later I realized that it dealt mostly with censorship and freedom of expression which are best treated as the right (or obligation!) to dissent. Ever since the invasion of the Golden Temple in 1984 and the subsequent news blackout by the Indian Government, I had been thinking about this question. Like many other Sikhs, I too had protested the Indian Government's control and manipulation of news from the Punjab under the guise of national security. But I must have been concerned about this issue far longer than I thought. I know that the Indian Government is not alone in this, all governments routinely try to control and manage news. We are all aware that in this country in the 1950s, many artists, authors and others were seriously harassed for their alleged links to communists; that period is now universally regarded as one of infamy. I had written against censorship when the Iranian Government condemned Salman Rushdie for blasphemy against Islam. And on my desk for the past twenty-five years or more has sat a bust of Galileo. (Galileo was finally forgiven by the Roman Catholic Church a month or so ago after 500 years in limbo and Rushdie may yet be spared by the mullahs of Iran if ever they are in a forgiving mood.)

My concerns here are more parochial. I had always prided myself on the fact that the Sikhs were very tolerant of dissent, even stupidity. Witness the nonsense about Guru Nanak, the founder of Sikhism, that was written by Dayanand, a Hindu *swami*, all because Nanak had been scornful of many Hindu practices and departed from the Hindu way. (Dayanand had freely and indiscriminately insulted not only Guru Nanak but the prophets of many other religions as well in his *magnum opus Satyarath Prakash.*) But Sikhs have not always been that tolerant, particularly since 1984 they have been increasingly narrow and bigoted in their interpretation of what is defamatory to their religion and how to respond to it. Fortunately, the Sikhs have been charitable to whatever I have written, the challenging voices have been few; others have not been so lucky.

Khushwant Singh, for instance, has been writing about Sikhs and Sikhism far longer than most of us have been around. He has some very credible writing in that area — translations of selections from the Sikh scriptures, an excellent two-volume history, and numerous articles. In defining Sikhism, he has attempted to place it squarely within the ancient Indian Vedantic, Hindu system, at other times he has deemed it an independent revealed, unique system. He is neither the first nor the last to be ambivalent. All these years the Sikhs respected him. Now that he is squarely against the idea of the Sikhs carving out a separate country independent of India, many Sikhs absolutely despise him. True that some of his ideas are blather and the trauma of 1984 to the Sikhs is deep. Yet, they forget that in 1984, Khushwant returned the honors bestowed upon him by the Indian Government and publicly declared that being a Sikh in India was like being a Jew in Nazi Germany. In any event, his writings on Sikhs and Sikhism need to be judged for themselves. I had occasion to review one of his books recently. I recognized the wit, pungency and style of his writing and called him an influential Sikh writer. Two U.S.-based prominent Sikhs berated me for calling him a 'Sikh.' To them, he was anathema and not fit to be labeled a Sikh. In reading him, the reader was to be pitied.

Patwant Singh, in my view, has emerged as a forceful voice for the Sikhs in India. Yet he does not fully support the idea of Khalistan. So, many Sikhs call him a stooge of the Indian

Government and have no use for his writings. One professor in India (Surjit Singh Chawla) recently wrote a book on Guru Tegh Bahadur's life and sacrifice. For some strange reason, the foreword is written by Giani Zail Singh, the former President of India, and most Sikhs equate Zail with Quisling for his role in the bloody events of 1984. It is a decent book but the foreword made it unacceptable to most Sikhs. It could not be selected for an international competition on book reports by Sikh youth. I would like to see the book debated, including the foreword. The young people would learn not only about Guru Tegh Bahadur but also a little about Giani Zail Singh and his failure to act as a *mensch*.

There is hardly a Sikh who is unaware of the arguments regarding McLeod and his writings. What bothers me is not the controversy; grown minds should be able to differ, and academicians routinely do. What irks me is the serious attempt to suppress his work, reject all that he has written, and a lot of it is good though some is not. For many reasons, McLeod has generated controversy and debate but little appreciation from the Sikhs. At times, he seems to have shed more heat than light on Sikh history. At issue are interpretations of many historical events. The early history of the Sikhs is a web so tangled that it is not easy to trace any strand unambiguously to its origin. Also, perusal of its early sources requires a mastery of many complex languages. This imposes a barrier to most scholars. I think McLeod's work marks a major systematic effort at an analysis of the evolution of the Sikhs from Guru Nanak to the twentieth century based on authentic historical documents and sources other than folklore. His work always carries a useful bibliography and raises significant issues. His writing is refreshing and lucid in its brevity and clarity, and free of the conceptual cobwebs and convoluted verbosity that often define 'religious' writing even though he has embraced some questionable if not erroneous concepts. I have little doubt that in peering past Sikh

traditions into history, McLeod has been touched by the depth
and richness of Sikh belief. Mind you, I am not here to defend
McLeod. Some of what he has written is nonsense but we need
not crucify him. He is neither the first nor the last with whom
we should and will differ in scholarly debate. Sikhism is too
strong and real to be defeated or lethally damaged by errors of
fact or interpretation by any writers; remember that it has lived
through the writings of Trumpp, Dayanand and Phillauri.

This brings me to the issue that provided the impetus for this
piece. Some weeks ago, I received a copy of a doctoral thesis by
Pashaura Singh on the antecedents of the *Guru Granth*. Several
scholars had already expressed highly critical opinions on it.
Yet, I agreed to review it because a wider debate could only
benefit us. It is only in the Sikh religion that a doctoral thesis is
debated and analyzed by the lay public and not only by
academicians in a scholarly, university-based journal.
Consequently, the discussion is open to all and not limited to
those affiliated with academic institutions. This is our strength
though it is not without liability. It is our strength because such
important matters are not left to the professional clergy or
academicians alone, it is our weakness for debate by unprepared
minds often leads to raised passions but not to clarity of thought.

That we may differ is a sacred right, almost a duty. But it is
a different matter when grave decisions are made without due
process, an attempt made to suppress the thesis and label it
blasphemous. For instance, the SGPC appears to have found
prima facie evidence of blasphemy by Pashaura Singh — all
without a hearing. Also, this is hardly a matter for the SGPC. I
too feel that Pashaura Singh is unable to sustain his hypothesis;
his evidence and logic are dubious and his loyalty to McLeod
misplaced, but those are matters to be debated by university
scholars, historians and theologians, as also by lay Sikhs. His
work can be termed sloppy scholarship but I fail to see the
notion of blasphemy in Sikh ideology. To attack his honesty,

integrity or his Sikh roots is not just irresponsible criticism, it borders on a grave obliviousness to the basic Sikh teachings on human dignity and freedom of expression.

It is not easy to separate the two but criticism of an idea must not become condemnation of the person who espouses it. In denouncing an idea, one must retain the moral high ground. A directive by the SGPC enjoining Sikhs not to read Pashaura Singh or Piar Singh takes me back to the days when the Roman Catholic Church compiled lists of books that a good Catholic may not read and movies that he must not see, otherwise a trip to the confessional box would be mandated. I think the Church stopped doing this a little over twenty years ago though not many Catholics were paying much mind to it for years earlier. For us to start on that road seems regressive. All that such policies do is to focus attention and give a new lease of life to something which normally would earn a quick burial in an unmarked grave. Certainly a lot more people read Salman Rushdie and Pashaura Singh after the publicity than would ever have; the only thing they have in common is that neither makes for notably good or interesting reading.

I understand that such an attempt by the SGPC is not new; decades ago it condemned some writing and ostracized the authors when it could. How is the suppression of a book by the SGPC any different from the censorship imposed by a government? The Indian Government has routinely done it and the Sikhs have universally condemned it every time. Is it possible that always being a part of the feudal Indian society, has so corrupted the SGPC that it can no longer see its own primary Sikh heritage very clearly?

Part of the problem lies in the fact that insofar as religions deal with historical events, people and places, they are amenable to historical analyses. But, religions also deal with a reality not clearly discernible to the outsider and which remains unfortunately hidden to the uninitiated. This essential essence of religion is such that our senses cannot perceive it, nor can our intellect fathom it, yet our souls can commune with it, for it transcends the intellect. Yet the intellectual, historical analysis enhances our understanding of a religion. Religions need to be viewed through the double lenses of faith and history. The single lens of history is inadequate, while that of faith alone often clouds the judgement. It follows then that the most effective commentators on a religion are scholars who are deeply touched by its inner reality, not others who are content to look at it as outsiders for they would be like those who, being anosmic, judge the fragrance of a flower only by a chemical analysis. For instance, reading Paul Tillich is a pleasure because his writings are not only intellectually rigorous but are also brimful of his commitment to Christianity; such wonder and joy would not exist in the writings of a mind with an anti-Christian stance. But how others view us is important and we need not be alarmed at their attempts.

In the past few years, a group of scholars seems to be emerging amongst Sikhs with the self-imposed task of being the watchdogs of what is published on or about Sikhism. I think that is good — more Sikhs should be so involved. A community has the right and the obligation to oversee the research that it is paying for. I am reassured that someone is minding the store except when an attempt is made to suppress what is deemed derogatory, defamatory or incorrect writing. To us Sikhs, *gurbani* is the revealed word of God but the *Guru Granth* is also a book, to be read and analyzed. To others, *gurbani* appears as literature, much as we view the Bible. And there is no harm in that.

Sikhism evolved in a milieu with a predominantly oral tradition but not much of a written one. Guru Nanak saw the necessity for a permanent written record which would evolve into the *Guru Granth Sahib*. He and the Gurus who succeeded him acted to preserve and codify *gurbani* in a process that culminated with Guru Arjan's monumental effort. Naturally, the process took years during which many versions and documents had to be edited or reconciled. One must keep in mind that in the days preceding printing and mass education, documents were handwritten. There were few scribes, some had their own agenda reflecting many factions and divided loyalties. They made mistakes, some unintentional, others stemming from their background, bias and nature. Until the time of Ranjit Singh, Sikhs had little peace or leisure, it is no wonder then that it took many years to lay all the doubts to rest, discard all of the competing or erroneous versions and establish the primacy of the standard version of the *Guru Granth Sahib* which had been collated by Guru Arjan. In the oral tradition of India, history and myth have frequently mixed. Naturally, historians will argue and ponder, reflect and debate when they look at the colorful panorama of Sikh history.

The Sikhs have come a long way in 500 years. I can visualize the rich tapestry and unbroken tradition in Sikh literature and history in its continuing evolution. It has progressed from giants such as Bhai Gurdas, Nandlal and Mani Singh, who were less historians and more scribes and interpreters of *gurbani*, indeed the repositories of our heritage. There have been Puran Singh, and Vir Singh who combined the mystic's vision with a sure grasp of historical detail. Finally, we have the serious historical scholars — giants like Kahan Singh, Macauliffe, Kapur Singh, Jodh Singh, Teja Singh, Ganda Singh, Sahib Singh and Harbans Singh, followed by contemporary, significant analysts like Kohli, McLeod, Khushwant, Cole, Barrier, Daljeet Singh, Kharak Singh, Mansukhani and Shan, among others. Such an evolution with an emphasis that oscillates between the devotional and the analytic is quite natural to any religion. In the process, many missteps will occur — witness G.B. Singh's analysis of the *Kartarpur Bir*, and some of the arrant nonsense from Trumpp, McLeod and Khushwant.

Not so long ago the radio commentator, Jodh Singh said to

me that we Sikhs tend to discover either 'blossom or blasphemy' in a strictly analytical study of religion. I think both attitudes are wrong ; one leads to suspended judgement and uncritical acceptance, the other to a Khomeni-like response to a Salman Rushdie. Neither becomes us for such attitudes are not consistent with Sikh teaching.

I believe the library in Alexandria was burnt twice, once by the Christians, another time by the Muslims because neither had any use for writings by those who were not 'true believers.' The whole idea of the First Amendment is that even a wrong opinion must not be censored; let it be buried by better ideas in the free marketplace of ideas. Erroneous ideas, even pernicious ones, are best countered by the fresh air of seminars, discussions and debates, not by suppression. History teaches us that ideas are hardly ever successfully buried by censorship. The lives of our Gurus are a testimony to that, as are those of Socrates, Galileo and Thomas More, among others. Spinoza, the Jewish philosopher who was excommunicated by the Jews for his ideas reminds us that those who do not remember their history are condemned to repeat it.

Nobody would deny that some restraint on freedom of expression may sometimes be necessary, but that is a grave and extreme step, not to be undertaken lightly. To refuse to read a book is one thing — that is a reader's right — to actively seek to suppress a book is no better than burning it. As I said, I keep a bust of Galileo on my desk.

Turn on, Tune in, Drop out

'Turn on, Tune in, Drop out' was an important incantation and message from the young in the sixties and I was a part of that generation. Man has had an age-old fascination with altered states of awareness and it doesn't date from the Beatles or Timothy Leary. The desire to transcend the constraints of human existence may be as old as man himself, and probably came with the gift of imagination. Not only has man learnt to soar beyond his physical limitations into outer space, he has also glimpsed an infinite universe within him. Having once tasted or seen that inner beauty, is it surprising that man looked for shortcuts? And found many.

Medical research tells us that meditation helps release certain intrinsic endorphins and phenylethylamine, a natural amphetamine — they serve as pain-killers and produce a euphoric high. Marathon runners and other intensively trained athletes have experienced it, as have those who experience intense feelings of love. When the physical, mental and spiritual parts of the self are in harmony and working in unison, that is when the production of these magic chemicals is at its greatest. There is a plethora of other biochemical changes too. That is the altered state of being that yogis have sought for ages, and so have those who experimented with mood-altering drugs as they sought shortcuts. When you attain it *a la* Leary, the highest high of euphoria is inevitably followed by a lowest low. With drugs, you cannot hit the mountain tops without trudging through the valleys.

With mood-altering drugs there is also a significant risk of

addiction or dependency, whether it be real physical depen-
dence or only psychological. Certainly the let-down — the low
— is dramatic, wrenching, painful and often debilitating. And
I won't even list the risks and hazards to self and to society that
can result. Those are the dangers of the extrinsic high. And that
doesn't take into account the fact that most mood-altering drugs
are also teratogenic — they result in an increased risk of fetal
defects. Witness the data on fetal alcohol syndrome or cocaine
or crack-addicted babies born to addicted mothers. Who knows
what are the effects of long-term usage of most habit-forming
substances on the body or mind? Modern medical science can
often be so tentative and ignorant, frustratingly unresponsive
and failing to provide definitive answers when we need them.

Guru Nanak, like other mystics also recognized the
pleasures of the high — the altered state of awareness — but he
also saw that the extrinsic drug-induced high was at best
transitory and had its attendant risks and perils. He sought,
therefore, a high which was available at your command, anytime
anyplace; which would last, be inexpensive and inexhaustible,
and leave your body and mind exalted, not exhausted.

Guru Nanak suggested a different mind-altering agent —
one for which you need no supplier for it costs nothing and the
supply never ends; it cannot be legislated or controlled. You can
have it when you want, carry it with you, and one that you do not
have to beg, borrow or steal. It produces a high which is greater
than any and has no low at all. But it is habit forming. This is
an intrinsic high, a glow from within. The intrinsic high is
qualitatively and quantitatively different from that produced by
extrinsic agents. This is the high produced by a life immersed
in an awareness of the infinite within us, an awareness that
connects man to God and his creation through *gurbani.*

Guru Nanak suggested two criteria for selecting how and
what to ingest or put into the human body. Several times in his
writings, he clearly recommended a life of moderation with no

taboos and also argued that any substance which is not good for the body or for the mind is *verboten*. The human body, in the Sikh view, is a temple within which is placed the divine spark of intelligence and the mind. We must ensure that whatever we do allows the body and mind to function at their highest levels.

With this kind of teaching, is it any wonder that Sikhism is adamantly against the use of any addictive, habit-forming, mood-altering drug of any kind? This does not mean that such drugs may not be available therapeutically in appropriate doses, for the right reasons, under suitable circumstances. It means that the use of the so called 'recreational' drugs cannot possibly be right; the word 'recreational' is inappropriate. Quite clearly, Sikhism could not condone the use of alcohol as commonly used, as a lubricant of social interaction. Without a doubt, it remains the commonest and most widely used addictive mind altering drug used in our society. The surprising thing is that despite this clear teaching, most Sikhs drink, if only just a little and socially. I too confess that I used to drink though not any more. We all want to appear socially sophisticated. In reality, refinement in lifestyle has less to do with what you drink or eat and more with how you do it. How did it happen that the use of alcohol among Sikhs did not get eradicated although another very pernicious habit — smoking — is practically never seen among them. Many factors may account for this. The most important reason may lie in the fact that the several codes of conduct that were written around the time of Guru Gobind Singh and soon thereafter clearly rejected the practice of smoking tobacco but are conspicuously silent on drinking alcohol. Then the question arises: why and how did that happen?

One must examine the Sikh writings on the code of conduct in the context of their times. The Indian society of that time was dominated by Muslims, though the majority of people were Hindus. Tobacco-smoking was commonly abused by both communities but drinking of alcohol was rare. The Muslims have strong injunctions against drinking, also they were the rulers. Although the Hindu scriptures speak of a fermented wine-like concoction, their society is generally a conservative one. In that society, drinking is not approved, appearing inebriated would not be easily forgiven, and never forgotten. In Sikhism, therefore, written injunctions are found against the common practice of the day — smoking — but not against the rarely seen abuse of alcohol. Now several hundred years later, when times have changed, we need to interpret and apply the written word with some sense and sensitivity; I think the code of conduct would now apply emphatically to all drugs and not specifically only to the one mentioned. Anyone can see that newer drugs continue to be found or synthesized and it would not be good logic to claim that since those new drugs are not mentioned in the code of conduct, there is no injunction against their abuse. The intent of the Gurus was quite clear — to create a community of dedicated, centred, people, healthy of mind and body. To interpret the teachings literally for one's own convenience is at best sophistry.

All that I have said can help understand Sikh teaching but not Sikh practice to any great extent. The fact remains that the countryside of Punjab is dotted with illicit distilleries. A running joke is that having lost some of the rivers to Pakistan at partition, Punjab, the land of the five rivers has added another river, that of alcohol. The Punjabi Sikh farmer is rarely hesitant or loath to brag about his prowess with the bottle. Part of this behavior is, of course, due to the narrow and literal interpretation of Sikh teaching. But a major part derives from history. Whether they were Aryans from the Caucuses of Asia Minor, Alexander of Macedonia or the Mughal hordes, most invaders to the fertile and rich plains of India came hurtling down the Khyber Pass into the Punjab — to stay, perish or return. This continuous influx produced a region and a people constantly in turmoil. The result was a vigorous, hybrid people constantly at war or, when time permitted, gifted farmers. Often, alcohol provided a welcome respite from a hard life. Only when the spiritual wave of Sikhism held strong sway over the hearts and minds of Punjabis, these illicit breweries were missing. This was also true when Islam reigned. But in time a gradual, lackadaisical Hinduization of Sikhs occurred. Such reversal into Hindu practices is not uncommon in India, where eventually everything and every idea from religion (Buddhism, Christianity, Islam or Sikhism) to industry gets Hinduized to some degree. Ties to Sikh teaching loosened. Over the past forty years, with the advent of the green revolution, the economy of the Punjab also dramatically boomed with few outlets for it. Consequently, the hard-working farmer and soldier of Punjab was easily seduced by the attractions of alcohol.

As further proof of my argument, I offer the fact that since 1984 (which marked a dramatic revolution in self-awareness for them), Sikhs have been on a voyage of self-exploration; the trek is nonlinear and sometimes seems to lead into blind alleys. However, many have rediscovered the richness of their faith and have again found the virtues of the Sikh code of conduct. The Sikh way of life is again being interpreted more honestly and less expediently. There will be many wrong turns but I am optimistic.

Keep in mind that the rich rarely feel compelled to follow any doctrinal mores, the poor cannot afford to. It is the middle class which is the repository of any culture and its values. And the middle-class Sikh is usually a fairly hard-working, reasonably religious, nonabuser of alcohol or other drugs. The loophole in Sikhism occurs because the onus for understanding the faith and following it falls on the individual. There is no hierarchy to correct any misinterpretations or parse any doctrinal differences. Some think that is a weakness of Sikhism but I think that is its strength. Who else but the individual should have the right and the obligation to think and decide which road to take? I would not want to abrogate that responsibility; to live ethically is my moral choice that I as a moral being must make. I would not want a professional clergy to force me on the straight and narrow; I would like the clergy to be there for me, to help and to guide me, as and when necessary.

Many mystics, including the Sikh Gurus have pointed out that our senses are limited in what they can perceive. As Buckminster Fuller suggests, our senses are designed to limit our perceptions. For instance, we cannot directly perceive radioactive fields, electromagnetic waves, etc. We cannot easily flow into and with the forces, circumstances and events that shape our universe, much of which remains infra or ultra to man's senses. Opening the doors of perception to what we do not normally perceive is a goal of meditation, as also of the drug-induced shortcut.

'Tune in, Turn on, Drop out' was an important slogan and exhortation. It was the *mantra* of the young in the sixties. But that related to the drug-induced experience. The message of the sixties is still relevant, the method is not and is rejected in its entirety. Guru Nanak accepted and taught the first two parts thus: turn on to the infinite within you and tune in to its infinite reality. Tune your mind to that infinite sense of peace, let it fill you and overwhelm you like fog creeping on silent feet, let it give you a rush. Start the day with a moment spent in quieting the mind before the madness of the day starts to overtake you. Say good morning to the world in peace. The third part has a different meaning in the writings of Sikhism. Do not drop out of the complex and infuriating demands of this world. Instead, be like a lotus that can emit beauty and fragrance and remain untouched by the stagnant water in which it may be found. Do not drop out to seek God on a mountaintop. Do not drop out to seek peace as a hermit or an ascetic. Live an active, productive, family life to serve God and society. But transcend the self, do drop out of the selfcentered existence, the ego trip which will only burn you. If you turn on, tune in and drop out this way, you will meet sorrow and joy, victory and defeat with equanimity ; you will know no fear nor will you bully or tyrannize another. Then you will be a man. This was the message of Nanak.

Nanak spoke of being constantly inebriated; the intoxicant was the love of God. The message of the sixties is not irrelevant ; it needs to be reinterpreted and tried as Nanak taught.

Some Thoughts on Racism and Sexism

There is hardly a Sikh who cannot recite from memory the lines from the *Guru Granth* which say: "In the beginning God created light, all creation and all creatures emanated from that one divine spark... All people are molded from the same clay...". But there is hardly a Sikh who takes the lines as seriously as he should in his life. To stratify society is natural, to divide people is inevitable. So easily and so universally does man divide men into 'us and them.' One hardly ever gives it a second thought except when it hits and hurts, when one is on the receiving end and is branded one of 'them.'

Over the years, many times I felt I like one of 'them' and not 'us.' But let me recount an event that made a more lasting impression. This happened some years ago when my daughter was only a couple of months old. Her mother's maternity leave was coming to an end and she needed to return to work. We started looking for an au pair girl and interviewed several young women. One very well-spoken person was a Jamaican black. The two grandmothers, one Indian, the other American, were aghast, their first reaction was: " Why this woman? She is so dark, she will scare the baby". Such color consciousness is probably universal in much of Europe and Asia. Just look at the advertisements for marriage partners in any Indian newspaper — they all look for brides or grooms who are fair in complexion. It appears from the these notices that lightness of color can make up for lack of education, skills or refinements. I wonder how a China doll would do in the Indian matrimonial market.

Our attempts to divide people doesn't just stop at color. The first question that our Hindu-dominated society wants to know is your caste and heaven help you if you are like me and refuse to give a straight answer to such irrelevant nonsense and invasion of privacy. My usual answer to what is your last name is, "Singh." I find this satisfies very few Indians. To most of them, the need to know the caste name is paramount. People persist and since I do not oblige them, I suppose I do not win many friends in the process. Look at how many Sikhs specify their caste, or at least whether they are Jats or not, when they advertise in the matrimonial columns.

My question is, if you are a Sikh, why and how is all this information relevant? The fact that such attitudes still exist three hundred years after Guru Gobind Singh created the egalitarian order of the *Khalsa* is not surprising. It would be more remarkable if they did not in the caste-ridden, hide-bound Indian society. The dominant Indian cultural tradition of Hinduism is extremely resilient. Almost like a sponge it can absorb an amazing lot without changing its own nature. The predominant cultural influence in India remains Hinduism and every idea that comes in contact with it becomes Hinduized. If Sikhism is no longer practiced the way it was taught, nor is any other religion particularly after it found roots in India; Christianity and Islam are prime examples. This obdurate resiliency in the Indian character remains its strength and also its most frustrating feature; it often proves a barrier to what is undesirable but also to what is progressive, and it corrupts all good ideas too. The latter has been the fate of Sikh thought.

Over two hundred years of very strong, clear-headed, single-minded teaching of the Sikhs from Nanak to Gobind Singh became diluted almost beyond recognition in the next three hundred years by the sponge of Indian Hindu cultural tradition. Believe me, I am not against the Indian culture. As a product of it, I know it to be a rich heritage and I value it, but not blindly.

Perfect, it is not. I would not want to build a life according to the Laws of Manu or establish a home by the teachings and practices of the Brahmins who are less than honorable shop-keepers of a less than an honest business.

Sikhism never had many adherents particularly because the religion was always being tested in battle. Almost from its birth, it has fought for survival, the wars were not always doctrinal. These battles for survival continue even today. The Sikhs have been opposed by the Brahmanical teaching of Hinduism and also by the established governments. There have been very few, relatively brief interludes of peace. The most important and longest such hiatus occurred when Ranjit Singh ruled northern India.

Millions of new converts flocked to Sikhism, most came from Hinduism (and some from Islam) during the time of Ranjit Singh. Their Sikhs roots were shallow; their conversion skin-deep, often one of convenience. Many brought with them practices and long-held beliefs of the predominant Hindu society such as the caste system and the place of women, and did not abandon them even though they were now Sikhs. Many of them who had been educated, upper-caste Hindus became influential in Sikh society. Perhaps without meaning to, they corrupted Sikh teaching and compromised Sikh practices. In fact, even Ranjit Singh's Sikh roots became watered down with the years as he ruled. Perhaps because the only role models for him were Muslim and Hindu rulers who had dominated India for so long, his personal lifestyle did not remain true to Sikh teachings for very long, although he supported Sikh gurdwaras. In the sea that is India, Sikhs constitute less than two percent of the population—a very small fish indeed. It is not surprising, therefore, that with time casteism, racism, sexism and color consciousness crept into Sikh practices, though every gurdwara preaches against them every day.

The young religion of Sikhism had laid great emphasis on

the responsible life of the householder, dedicated to honest work ethic and service to fellow man. Yet, when the opportunity came, Ranjit Singh, otherwise noble of character and a dedicated ruler, took several hundred queens and concubines; several of his queens committed *suttee* when he died. Multiple marriages in Islam were permissible. In Hinduism, women never had a very important place; they were not allowed to read scriptures, if widowed they were expected to burn themselves at the pyre of their dead husband, or if not that, to remain single thereafter. Clerical, religious functions were not open to women in either of two more populous religions, Islam or Hinduism. Sikhs had been egalitarian from the very beginning, rejecting racism, casteism and sexism forthrightly. Sikhs define God as free of gender, do not use the attributes 'He' or 'She' for God or use both terms interchangeably. If we often seem to use 'He' in preference to 'She', it is reflective of custom and the limitations of imagination, thought and language, not of Sikh teaching.

However, for reasons alluded to, Sikh practices have departed from their teaching in significant ways. Some years ago, when I briefly served as the Program Secretary of our local gurdwara, I requested the oldest lady in the congregation to sit at the altar and lead the congregation in the prayer. These functions are not restricted to the clergy in Sikhism and are often performed by lay people. That day, some people from the local press were visiting. I thought rather than subject them to a boring, unwelcome lecture on the equal place of women in Sikhism, I would show it by having a woman lead the congregation. The function went smoothly but afterwards some Sikhs wanted to know — why a woman?

When Guru Gobind Singh gave the Sikhs their present form 300 years ago, he challenged his followers to offer their heads. After much confusion and consternation, five men stepped up. They were the first five baptized or confirmed Sikhs, the sixth one was Guru Gobind Singh himself. From then on, tradition has it that the *Amrit* ceremony of confirmation requires five *Amritdhari* Sikhs in attendance. By convention, they have been male, I have never seen a woman among those five, though many women receive *Amrit.* When not so long ago, one woman in New York wanted to be one of those five, the *granthi* of a local gurdwara objected. On what grounds, I still fail to understand except that the first five were men. Such reasoning (or lack thereof) reminds me of the Roman Catholic logic on why a nun could not perform all of the priestly functions — because Jesus and the apostles were males. Given the clarity of Sikh teaching, I would have to label such thinking regressive and asinine. If the first five converts were male, the reason is not much different from why none of the Gurus was a female. It has more to do with circumstances, the times and the society in which we functioned then and now, and little to do with Sikh teaching.

Sikhism promised an equal place to women. The predominant society then and now does not; therefore, the practice fell far short of the preaching. In many matters, however, Sikhism delivered. For instance, the Sikh Gurus were the first to raise their voices against *suttee*, a truly abominable custom. Widow remarriage was instituted by the Sikhs. There is no activity in the Sikh religion reserved exclusively for men, nor is there any which is closed to them. This is important to note because in many religions a woman may not read the scriptures, lead the prayers or perform many of the other priestly functions, particularly if she is menstruating. There is no ritual purification ceremony required of her once a month. If in a Sikh service, men and women sit on separate sides, it is based on custom, culture and tradition, not canon. When the widespread Sikhs were organized into twenty-two diocesan centres by Guru Amar Das, many of the directors were women. In Sikh history, women have led armies into battle.

There is no question that sexism is un-Sikh and that the two genders share equally, enjoying the same rights, privileges and miseries. Once again this is clearly brought home by the fact that in the first names of Sikhs, no sexual distinction or identification is traditionally made. Only 'Singh' or 'Kaur' are used to distinguish a male name from that of a female. The traditional first name is absolutely gender-neutral. The use of gender-specific first names among Sikhs is a relatively recent phenomenon; the trend seems to be a reflection of the predominant non-Sikh culture around us. Except as responsible ethical individuals, the roles that men and women play in life are not defined by Sikh names, teachings or ceremonies but are determined by their own individual circumstances. The Gurus saw that often time, culture and individual circumstances shape what we do; if the people are responsible and ethical, they will evolve behaviors that are neither masochistic nor exploitive or sexist.

On matters of racism, sexism, etc, Sikh teaching could not be more explicit and less ambiguous. Yet, it is in these matters that I find Sikh teaching and Sikh practice to show the widest divergence. I can look back in history when the two lines were inseparable; when I look further into the future, I do not know when the two will meet again — that they will, I know.

Ecological and Environmental Concerns in Sikhism

The exploration of space in the twentieth century has afforded us a unique perspective of our existence and of our environment. A revolution in science was started by Copernicus at about the same time that Nanak was starting a spiritual revolution in self-awareness. Both revolutions, progressing apace, still incomplete, define man's place in God's creation.

Science today echoes the vision of Nanak 500 years ago. Nanak spoke of solar systems without end, a universe that defies description and lies beyond human comprehension. In the Sikh world view, God is the creator of all and is revealed through His creation — a creation which transcends man's instruments, his philosophies, his space voyages and defies his measurements. Nanak speaks of "Hundreds of thousands of worlds 'neath and o'er ours; Scholars fail to define God's bounds...". In very direct but surprisingly modern idiom, Guru Nanak speaks not just of this universe but many more - innumerable galaxies, beyond human comprehension. Guru Nanak clearly refutes any claims as to the time, day or year of creation, and speaks of the void that preceded creation.

It is into such a creation that God has placed man with a divine spark of intelligence and the power to redesign and utilize God's creation for his ends. But to redesign towards what ends and for what purposes? Nanak's reverence for life, for nature and for God's creation is illustrated by his many writings such as: "Air — the breath of life; Water — the progenitor; Earth — the universal mother." At another time Nanak said: "True are thy universes; Holy thy worlds and creation; Holy thy actions; True thy decree". A somewhat similar thought is expressed in the *Old Testament* (Psalms xix, 1): "The heavens above declare the glory of God. The firmament below shows his handiwork."

The environmental crisis facing mankind can be gauged by the simple statistic that over 20 billion tons of waste a year — much of it effluent from factories, homes and farms — end up in the sea. Also, a town like Delhi has lost 60 percent of its forest cover within a decade as a result of its growing demand for fuel. (For illustration, I pick Delhi and not New York because for many reasons the crisis in developing countries is even more horrendous; they cannot neglect industrial development, yet to underestimate the future repercussions of poor environmental policies now will be foolish.)

It is now easy to easy to see what the Sikh attitude towards the current ecological and environmental crisis should be. The emphasis of Sikh teaching is not in the laying down of highly precise, rigid, unchanging and specific rules of how man might utilize God's creation, including his fellow beings on mother earth. These technical matters would require technical expertise and decisions made by scientifically trained minds with a highly sophisticated base of knowledge. And what we decide today will change tomorrow based on new information. The essence of Sikh teaching is to provide man with a healthy, progressive, forward-looking and responsible philosophy to guide human actions so that decisions are intelligently and ethically made.

The Guru recognized that existence is a strange bargain; life owes us little, we owe it everything. It follows then that if air or '*pavan*' is Guru, the life-giving force, it would be sinful to pollute it; if water or '*pani*' sires us and earth is mother, dumping our garbage into our rivers would be unforgivable. Guru Nanak in his writings was celebrating what Keats called "the poetry of earth".

In the lives of quiet desperation that humans lead, what

ethical values to give to man in a manner that is both simple and universal, yet effective at the same time? Guru Nanak addressed these issues very directly and forthrightly. While exhorting man not to renounce the world but to meet its challenges squarely, not to shun progress but to pursue it responsibly, the Guru gave guidelines for what constitutes responsible living.

Sikhism teaches against a life of conspicuous, wasteful consumption. The Guru taught man to be aware of and respect the dignity in all life, whether human or not. Such a respect for life can only be fostered where one can first recognize the divine spark within oneself, see it in others, cherish it, nurture and fulfill it. Translated into easily understood terms: to spend a life which depends for its existence on an honest job honestly done (the work ethic), the rewards of such a life to be shared with others to inculcate a sense of giving of oneself and social responsibility, and all this is to be done with an awareness of the Infinite within one.

A life dedicated to such a philosophy, Sikhism asserts, would address both the internal environmental crises of man's spirit and the external environmental crisis of mother earth caused by man's spiritual emptiness and irresponsibility. Sikhs believe that the environmental crisis is primarily and fundamentally spiritual in nature. An awareness of man's symbiotic relationship to mother earth, air, water — in fact, to his total environment is necessary. Life, for its very existence and nurturing, depends upon a bounteous nature. Man needs to derive sustenance from the parent, not to deplete, exhaust, pollute, burn or destroy it. Sikhs believe that an awareness of that sacred relationship between man and the environment is necessary for the health of our environment and this planet, and for our own survival. A new 'environmental ethic' can only arise from an honest understanding and dedicated application of our old, tried and true spiritual heritage.

Epilogue

These days, most Sikhs that I meet seem to have a beef; they think that the world has done them wrong. They express considerable bewilderment, frustration, impatience and a sense of impotence with the dichotomy between how we view ourselves and how others see us, particularly those who have very little knowledge of us. The gulf has widened considerably since 1984 when the Indian Army attacked the Golden Temple and forty other gurdwaras across the Punjab. The problem has been exacerbated by the relentless campaign of the Indian Government which has used its massive resources in a worldwide campaign to portray the Sikhs as terrorists hell-bent on fragmenting India. If many Sikhs appear shell-shocked, there is plenty of good reason for it.

Whether they are educated or barely literate, most Sikhs are justifiably proud of their heritage, their young religion, and the achievements of their people. Yet, they say, "The world knows so little of us and what it does know is often wrong — colored by the Indian Government's propaganda." How is it, they want to know, that we have not been able to show the world the beauty, majesty and richness of our religion? Why is it that the world knows so little or cares even less about us and our fate?

The rage and frustration are understandable but, I submit, such feelings are not entirely justified. Let us not be too hard on ourselves.

Do not forget that the Sikh religion is young ; 500 years in terms of history is not even a drop in the bucket. Our numbers are minuscule, there are about as many Sikhs as there are Jews.

The British are wrongly blamed for many of the ills of Indian society, but in one matter they could really share some. When the British came to India, they brought their own worldview and philosophy. The outwardly obsequious Indian mind resented it but learnt to ape an alien language, culture and tradition. And necessarily neglected and devalued its own. Survival demanded the former, the latter became inevitable. At least partially at fault is the traditional Indian system of education in which the mind is viewed as an empty bucket to be filled. The teacher speaks, the student listens — no ifs or buts. The great gift of Western philosophic tradition to mankind is the Socratic method which depends on 'ifs and buts' to awaken and stretch the mind.

More importantly, we represent perhaps the first generation of Sikhs with the availability of nearly universal education in both our traditional lore as well as the western modes of communication. In our fathers' days, Sikh college graduates were few and far between. Less than two generations ago, our forefathers ran modest businesses in small towns or were farmers. Their education was limited to a smattering of the mother tongue and some instruction in the scriptures. They were just as innocent of the rest of the world as the world was of them. To some extent the First World War and later the second, provided them the first opportunities to expand their horizons. It is good to remember that from the time of the Gurus until the dawn of the twentieth century, the imperatives of survival were such that the Sikhs knew very little peace and leisure except briefly during Ranjit Singh's reign. War and repressive governments dominated their existence far too long but shaped their indomitable spirit.

Our generation which grew up primarily after 1947 has enjoyed prosperity in the Punjab, widespread education, opportunities to travel, and unheard of ways to broaden the mind. Prior to this time, our contacts with the world outside

Punjab were limited.   Many of this new generation have
successfully grafted the western-oriented, outer-directed,
exploratory attitude to life on to their own Sikh heritage,
because the two have always been quite compatible.

For the past forty years or so, we have been under siege in
India, more so since 1984. Yet these years have seen a remarkable growth in literature on or about the Sikhs by Sikhs and
others. Universities and Colleges in India have sprouted
academic programs with a focus on Sikhs Studies. I point
particularly to the number of Khalsa Colleges and Sikh institutions as well as to the establishment of Guru Nanak Dev and
Punjabi Universities in India within the past twenty-five years.
Even outside India, particularly in Great Britain and North
America, departments and academic activities on Sikhs Studies
have burgeoned. Conferences on Sikh Studies have been
hosted by the University of California and new Sikh Studies
programs have been developed at Columbia University as well
as the Universities of British Columbia, Toronto and Michigan.
Books and newspapers that highlight Sikh concerns are published and widely distributed. Some of what is new is also
nonsense and may not survive. But time will separate the wheat
from the chaff.

The past twenty years or so have seen a quantum leap in the
number of academic programs in hitherto neglected areas; look
at the growth of Black Studies, Islamic Studies, Hebraic Studies
and Women Studies, for example. It is time that Sikh Studies
emerged to take its rightful place alongside these new academic
disciplines. The domain of Sikh Studies is a newly developing
one; the dimension of this fledgling yet to be defined, but it is
a vigorous product of a vibrant people. We are still learning —
our Vedantic roots, our semitic antecedents, our revealed,
unique religion of the Book — but we are greater than the sum
of the parts. We are still learning to disagree amongst ourselves
without being disagreeable. A new world requires new strate-

gies and tactics, a new armory of the mind. And we are learning.

There are also other indications of growing self-awareness. This year I received many New Year cards with a Sikh motif, more than ever before; only a few years ago, such cards would have been impossible to find in the market. Television and radio in many cities outside India offer programming from a Sikh point of view; these would have been unthinkable only a few years ago. In the area of human rights, the U.S. Congress and Amnesty International have taken note of the Indian Government's lawlessness and state-sponsored terrorism in the Punjab. Many young Sikhs escaping the horrors in India have been granted political asylum in the United States in the past few years.

Christianity and Islam flourished because of political patronage in their heyday. The Jews have honed their skills during two thousand years of suffering, have had centuries of contacts with Europe which was dominant both politically and economically, and have a state. Remember that no country or government speaks for us. We are still young. We are the new kids on the block.

If we are dissatisfied with where we are, it only means that our goals are higher than our grasp, and that is as it should be. T.S. Eliot reminds us,

> *Between the conception*
> *And the creation*
> *Between the emotion*
> *And the response*
> *Falls the shadow*
> *Life is very long.*

Let us not be too harsh or impatient with ourselves. To Sikhs, I would say somewhat irreverently, "You have come a long way, baby." I should add "You have a longer way to go."

Glossary

Amrit

Sikh initiation roughly comparable to the rite of confirmation in Christianity, and introduced by Guru Gobind Singh in 1699. Those who receive *Amrit* are called *Amritdhari* and accept the lifestyle and symbols of the *Khalsa*.

Anand Karaj

Literally 'sacrament of joy.' It is the Sikh marriage ceremony.

Babri Mosque

A mosque in Ayodhya built by the Moslem king Babar who ruled India in the sixteenth century. Hindus contend that it occupies the exact site where their god-king Rama was born.

Bhagvad Gita

Sacred book of Hindus. Contains the teachings of Krishna.

Brahma

One of the trinity of Hindu gods. The supreme creative spirit in Hinduism.

Brahmin

The highest, priestly caste among the Hindus. Historically, only males of this hereditary caste are allowed to perform Hindu sacred rites.

Chappatties

Flat bread, usually unleavened. Staple of Punjabi food.

Dasam Granth

Many but not all of the writings in this compilation are attibuted to Guru Gobind Singh. They are not included in the *Guru Granth*.

153

Durga	Consort of Shiva. Usually depicted with eight arms and a garland of skulls. Embodiment of power in Hinduism.
Ghadar Party	A political association of Indians, largely Punjabi Sikhs, based in California and British Columbia active in the early years of the twentieth century against the British occupation of India.
Granthi	Scholar or curator of the *Guru Granth*, usually in charge of a gurdwara.
Gurbani	Teachings of the Gurus and saints as enshrined in the *Guru Granth*. Loosely interpreted, it often means not only the content of the *Guru Granth* but also the writings of Guru Gobind Singh (*Dasam Granth*), Bhai Gurdas and Bhai Nand Lal.
Gurdwara	Sikh house of worship. Analogous to a temple, mosque or a church.
Guru Granth	Guru Arjan compiled the main body of the text in 1604 as the *Adi Granth*. It contains the writings of the Sikh Gurus as well as of Moslem and Hindu saints, some of whom were from the lower castes of Hinduism. Guru Gobind Singh added the writings of Guru Tegh Bahadur and installed this sacred scripture of the Sikhs' as the living guru.
Halal	Flesh from an animal slaughtered in the ritual way according to Islamic teaching. Akin to kosher meat in Judaic practice.
Imam	A scholar of Islamic religion.
Indra	Hindu Vedic god of rain and thunder. Protector of cows, priests and other lesser gods.

Karma	The concept of eventual justice. It contends that everything that happens is preordained, according to one's actions in an earlier life. A cornerstone of Hindu philosophy.
Katha	Exposition of Sikh scriptural writing or heritage during a Sikh religious service, in the presence of the *Guru Granth.*
Keertan	Singing of the liturgy in a Sikh religious service.
Keshadhari	Sikhs who maintain the five external symbols of Sikhism. Not all *keshadhari* Sikhs are *Amritdhari.*
Lakshmi	Consort of Vishnu, goddess of wealth in Hinduism.
Langar	A meal prepared by volunteers and served to all irrespective of their religious beliefs after a Sikh religious service. Many gurdwaras serve *langar* twice a day, others have continuous *langar* available at any time of the day. Men and women vie for the opportunity to serve and the people are seated randomly without regard to status, caste, etc. This breaks the usual Hindu restrictions of caste.
Manu	Scholar and law-giver of Hinduism, the final authority in Hindu law. He codified many of the Hindu rituals and practices, including those of the caste system and the place of women. Lived perhaps between 600 and 200 B.C.
Namdharis	A small subsect of Sikhs. They believe all of the teachings of Sikhism except

one: whereas, the majority of Sikhs believe that Guru Gobind Singh vested the *Guru Granth* with all spiritual authority, the *Namdharis* look to a Guru in human form to guide them.

Patit

Literally an apostate. Used in a derogatory manner for Sikhs who follow Sikhism as their religion, were once at least *Keshadhari* if not *Amritdhari*, and now do not maintain long unshorn hair. Technically, a *Patit* Sikh is he who, having committed a cardinal sin against Sikh teaching, is no longer in a state of grace.

Ramayana

A Hindu epic detailing the trials, tribulations and triumphs of their god-king Rama.

Sangat

Also called *Sadh Sangat.* Literally, a congregation united in holy purpose or prayer.

Sehajdhari

Sikhs who follow Sikhism as their religion except that they were never initiated by *Amrit* into the *Khalsa* and never maintained long unshorn hair, the most visible external symbol of the Sikhs. They are to be distinguished from the *Patit* Sikhs.

Sevadar

Literally, one who serves. It is the traditional term in Punjabi for an officer of the gurdwara or a Sikh organization.

S.G.P.C.

Shiromani Gurdwara Prabandhak Committee, a Sikh organization which supervises the administration of historic gurdwaras all over India. Came into existence in 1922 by an Act of the Government of India after the Sikhs wrested control of their gurdwaras from the British Government following a massive agitation.

Shiva One of the trinity of Hindu gods. The supreme spirit of destruction in Hinduism.

Suttee A Hindu custom in which a widow was burnt at the cremation pyre of her dead husband. Finally outlawed by the British, it is still occasionally seen. The widow is referred to as *Sati*.